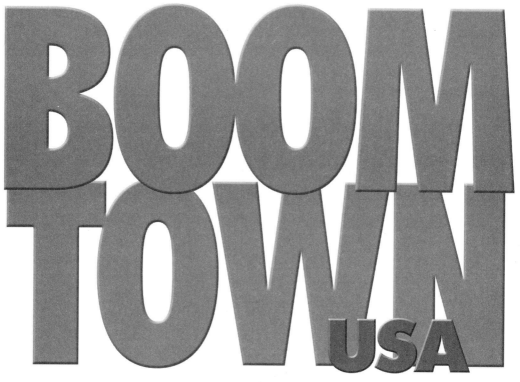

BOOM TOWN USA

THE **7½ Keys**
TO BIG SUCCESS
IN SMALL TOWNS

TO DONNA:
I LOVED PRESCOTT! It is A
WONDERFUL Golden EAqle.

Jack Schultz

Jack Schultz

D0451549

naiop
National Association of
Industrial and Office Properties

Library of Congress Cataloging-in-Publication Data

Schultz, John M., 1952–
    Boomtown USA: the 7-1/2 keys to big success in small towns / by John M. Schultz.
        p. cm.
    Includes bibliographical references and index.
    ISBN 0-9718955-2-X
    1. Industrial promotion—United States. 2. Industrial policy—United States. 3. Urban economics—United States. 4. Community development, Urban—United States. I. Title.

    HC110.153S38 2004
    338.973'009173'2—dc22

                                                                2003071067

Cover design by Estasi Design Associates. Photograph of Leavenworth circa 1950s courtesy of Leavenworth Chamber of Commerce. Photograph of Columbus City Hall courtesy of Balthazar Korab LTD.

National Association of Industrial and Office Properties

2201 Cooperative Way

Herndon, VA 20171

www.naiop.org

Printed in the United States of America

ISBN 0-9718955-2-X

Dedication

To Betinha, James, Joseph and Team Agracel,
You are the best!
You are "Can Do" in action.

Contents

Acknowledgments vii

Introduction ix

CHAPTER 1
The Dilemma and the Opportunities.. 1

CHAPTER 2
Back to the Agurbs... 7

CHAPTER 3
Key #1: Adopt a Can-Do Attitude.. 25

CHAPTER 4
Key #2: Shape Your Vision 41

CHAPTER 5
Key #3: Leverage Your Resources 55

CHAPTER 6
Key #4: Raise Up Strong Leaders... 69

CHAPTER 7
Key #5: Encourage an Entrepreneurial Approach......................... 83

CHAPTER 8
Key #6: Maintain Local Control 93

CHAPTER 9
Key #7: Build Your Brand..101

CHAPTER 10
Key #7½: Embrace the Teeter-Totter Factor.................................. 111

CHAPTER 11
Case Study: Making All the Keys Work..119

CHAPTER 12
Comparing Agurbs and Cities 131

CHAPTER 13
A Look into the Agurban Future..137

Appendix A: Agurbs in the U.S.A. 143

Appendix B: Local Flavor of Towns..161

Index 169

Bibliography..181

Acknowledgments

*B*oomtown USA: The 7½ Keys to Big Success in Small Towns would not have been possible without the valuable assistance and support of many people. A special thank you to writer Tom Hanlon, who provided invaluable assistance in helping me put my ideas into words. He is a gem! My agent, Marta Justak, took a chance on an unproven author and passionately embraced a vision of our boomtowns and provided much more value than I'll ever be able to repay. Both Sheila Vertino and Shirley Maloney of NAIOP were enthusiastic in their support of this project, provided great editorial oversight and guided us throughout.

This book project would not have happened without the urging and support of the small group of people whom I am very fortunate to work alongside. Team Agracel wouldn't accept my excuses of why this project wouldn't work; instead, in their typical "Can-Do" fashion, they just told me to do it. I am thankful that they picked up some of my daily load, provided great ideas for the book and continue to be an inspiration to me on a daily basis.

My partners at Agracel: Dean Bingham, who sits next to me every day, allowing us to bounce ideas off of each other. He isn't afraid to tell me when an idea is nuts! He is a soul mate sharing my passion for small towns. Dick Lumpkin is my mentor and the most generous person I have ever met. Steve Grissom is the best sounding board I've ever had. They and Mary Lee Sparks all very generously offered to underwrite this entire project.

At Agracel, Coleen Phillips coordinated this entire project and kept me on track. Lisa Huston painstakingly researched and documented each of the facts and stories in this book. Lynn Higgs kept a lot of balls in the air while maintaining a great sense of humor. I also want to thank at Agracel: Sharon Harper, Jeff Bloemker, Janet Grunloh, Mike Cluck, Steve Sims, Todd Thoman, Mike French, Frank Bock, Theresa Schackmann, Theresa Daniels, Jim Jobe, Mike Mumm, Rob Powell, Mike Zeller, Josh Storck, Kacie Volpi, Steve Brandenburg, Bob Carnahan, Justin O'Dell, Terri Elder, Mike Shoot, Sarah Robins,

Kathie Koontz, Andy Foster, Doug Hall and Jarrad Phillips. Thanks for your support, especially on my occasional Don Quixote project.

I want to thank Rick Siemer, Hank Stephens, Mike Kearney, P. J. Ryan and Donna Riley-Gordon, who read early drafts of the book and provided valuable ideas and insight into the development of small towns. I also want to thank John Mehner, the head of the Chamber of Commerce in Cape Girardeau, Missouri, who set up several days of meetings with the key players in that great town and provided great information on the community.

Seventeen years ago, when I started on a quest of doing economic and industrial development in small towns—a rather small niche—I was encouraged by a number of people without whose support it might never have happened. Very early partners, Jim Schultz and the late Fred and Polly Hale, believed in what we were doing and took a chance with us. Bud Althoff, Jack Thies, Dale Fitzpatrick and Mort Rosen allowed us to do our first industrial project, while Howard Atkinson allowed an important, second one that really highlighted our process. A special thank you to our early investors who had faith we would make these first projects work: Dean Samuel, the late Nick Dust, Bob Schultz, Ann Deters, Ron Sippel and Paul Grunloh.

A special thank you to Charlie Barenfanger, our partner on the Effingham Railroad, who taught our entire team the beauty of the rails. Without his leadership, fortitude and dedication we would never have gotten that important project built.

My parents, Fran and the late John Schultz, and in-laws, Mary Lee and the late Pete Emmert, have always been very encouraging. Each of you provided an inspiration to me with your joy of life, direction and strong moral compass. Mom, thanks for inspiring me with your writing of columns, articles and books.

Betinha, my wife of 23 years, is my rock. She is a thoroughbred filly who settled for a plow horse, and I am grateful. I'll remember to take the trash out, throw my dirty clothes in the hamper and unload the dishwasher now that this project is done. To our sons, James and Joseph, you inspire me each day with your "Can-Do" approach to life.

Jack Schultz
Effingham, Illinois

Introduction

As CEO of a company whose mission, in part, is to develop business in small towns, I have interacted with hundreds of business executives and town officials in the Midwest, primarily in Iowa and Minnesota. I have often felt like a detective looking for clues to answer several questions about small-town health and prosperity: What separates the thriving towns from the struggling ones? Do the people within a prosperous town approach their lives differently than those in a struggling town? Can communities that are struggling rebound? If so, how?

Questions like these prompted me to explore the roots of success in small towns. As I dug deeper, I found the roots of small-town success intertwined with the roots of individual success. I observed the resurgence of some, and the slow death of many, small towns. These observations piqued my curiosity. I wanted to fully understand why some communities were growing and offering opportunities to their young people, while others were turning into ghost towns.

I started out feeling that what I was seeing was not unique to any particular town. There are certain commonalities among the successful towns that contrast them tremendously from what I call the Hayseedvilles of the world. Some town residents exude a vibrancy, a self-assurance and a conviction that their town is special. I can usually tell this by driving into town and stopping to talk with someone from the chamber of commerce or with the town economic developer. I knew, as I traveled around the Midwest and met with folks from various towns, which communities were healthy and which weren't. But it was difficult to quantify why.

At the same time, I saw a national demographic trend emerging: People were moving to small towns primarily for quality of life issues. While not a tidal wave, this trend appears likely to continue for many years and, indeed, has caught the attention of futurists who address not only *how* we will live in the 21st century but also *where* we will live.

The Personal Perspective

I didn't have to drive around the Midwest to study a small town in crisis. The economic woes of my own town, Effingham, Illinois, presented more than enough crises to not only study, but to roll up my sleeves and actively participate in its reparation. In fact, my company—Agracel, Inc.—got its beginnings just as Effingham came face-to-face with its economic crisis in 1988; the town's predicament helped define my company's focus on economic development.

Effingham faced a loss of 3,000 of its 4,000 manufacturing jobs as its three largest manufacturers were on the verge of closing or moving out of town. As these plans became public, community response ranged from shock to anger to panic to depression, depending on whom you talked to. A paralysis born of fear began to settle over the town like a fine dust as Effingham considered its uncertain future.

I joined a small group of concerned citizens—including the mayor, several bankers, some plant managers, the city economic developer, a real estate agent, and some retirees—who met many times over the next several months to discuss the downhill slide of our town. From those meetings a general consensus evolved: We could no longer depend on just a few companies, no matter how good those companies were. We had to diversify our base of jobs. We had to attract multiple, and generally smaller, plants, so that if a few closed they would not cripple the community's economy.

The town hired a marketing group to help restore its image. Articles were placed in a variety of publications, including the *Chicago Tribune* and *Newsweek*. Local high school students became an integral part of a telemarketing campaign to prospective companies. Out of a community-wide planning session came a town slogan: Crossroads of Opportunity. These efforts began to change the local residents' attitudes and feelings about the town.

The coffee shop talk turned from a hand-wringing "woe is me" into an attitude that these temporary setbacks would be overcome. Gradually, Effingham developed a positive image and a brand for itself, as its 10,000 residents turned into town ambassadors (See Chapter 9 for a thorough discussion of branding). No companies came to town as a direct result of any of this—but through these efforts the community began to recover its spirit, enthusiasm and optimism. The town began to feel good about itself again. It began to exhibit a "Can-Do" attitude, which, as I'll explain in Chapter 3, is the first step to success.

Effingham began recruiting high-tech and manufacturing companies that would offer between 100 and 300 jobs. More than five years passed before the first manufacturer decided to build a new plant. But, once that first one made the leap, companies such as Coca-Cola, Pepsi, Krispy Kreme, Bunge Foods and others located new facilities in Effingham. That first manufacturer (which is no longer in business), started a chain reaction of one company after another locating in our town. Not all of the companies that started operations succeeded, but the majority did, and employment grew greatly within the town. In fact, during the 1990s, Effingham realized a 70 percent increase in new manufacturing jobs, leading all Illinois counties in this category.

Effingham's story is only one of hundreds among small towns that have either rebounded to health and vitality or have maintained their strength and position. Prosperous small towns abound in every region of the country and in every state; oddly enough, they often are a stone's throw away from a town that is dying on the vine.

Small Towns, Agricultural Roots

Virtually every small town mentioned in this book has some tie-in to agriculture. Most started as agricultural centers and gradually developed from those roots. My company, Agracel, began in the agricultural arena and evolved into industrial development in small towns. When that facet of our business began to take off, we struggled with renaming ourselves to better reflect industrial development. But after reviewing a number of names we asked ourselves, "What are farmers?"

Farmers are down-to-earth people who must master cutting-edge technology in a very tough business. They survive on razor-thin margins, must react instantly to unpredictable changes, control their resources meticulously and constantly innovate to solve problems and improve their operations. Farmers build long-term relationships. They treat their land as a long-term steward, concerned about the next generation and generations after.

The farm is probably the most efficient unit we know of. Farmers are cross-trained, fully functional and multifaceted. Everyone helps one another. And you can't fake farming. Crops either grow or they don't. Farms don't have bureaucracies: When they have a problem, they solve it. Decisions are made easily and quickly. Deals are done on handshakes. After looking at it from that perspective, we decided to keep the name Agracel.

Identifying Common Characteristics

As I worked in Effingham and with towns throughout the Midwest, my "detective work" began to pay off. Through my travels and business consultations, the research I conducted, and my observations in working with many business owners and executives, public officials and concerned citizens, I began to discover the reasons that certain towns thrive while others do not. I delved into the data for small towns, starting in Illinois. I then expanded the quest into a national one, looking at trends from the 2000 U.S. Census. Based on the census information, I narrowed the list of more than 15,800 small towns to 1,300.

My feeling about what distinguished successful towns from the average ones became first a theory, then a conviction. I continually saw the same characteristics, from one great town to another. These characteristics by themselves weren't earth-shattering. Considered together, however, they began to build a case for exactly how successful small towns set themselves apart, often by a wide margin. The keys to success, which emerged over time, don't form a magic wand; they can't resuscitate a near-dead town within a few weeks or even months. But they can lead to significant improvement in a town's economy and growth.

People in vibrant and healthy small towns are already operating in ways that perpetuate their own, and their town's prosperity, but no one had taken the time to tell others how to function in a like manner. No one had expressed to them the keys to successful small-town development.

Until now.

What It Takes

The time has never been riper for small communities to prosper. Deregulation of numerous industries—trucking, airlines and many more—works in favor of small communities. Operating costs for businesses and corporations are lower in small-town settings. The increasing ease and affordability of how we communicate with one another, and how we travel to meet with each other, no longer make living in large cities a necessity for doing business. Small communities typify the rural work ethic and provide a ready and willing labor force. The charms of living in a vibrant small town are legendary and real; many people move to small towns for quality of life issues, including better education, more affordable housing, less crime, a better environment and a shortened commute to work. These are just some of the myriad reasons that rural communities are capable of prospering.

But that prosperity doesn't happen on its own.

It happens through solid and visionary leadership, having a "Can-Do" attitude and exhibiting a willingness to take risks. It happens through knowing what your town's strengths and resources are and how to leverage those strengths and resources. It happens through building a brand for your town— a concept that often prompts quizzical looks, yet one that successful small towns have embraced.

Within these pages I share what I have learned over the past 15 years about small-town prosperity. I also identify what I consider the top 397 (and within them, the top 100) small communities in America. These communities by themselves run the risk of getting lost among the more than 15,800 small towns in rural America. But a closer look at these prosperous communities reveals that they have astounding strengths.

Agurbs is a term I coined for these communities to distinguish them from all the other small towns in rural America. What exactly is an agurb?

An agurb is a prospering rural town with a tie to agriculture and a location outside a Metropolitan Statistical Area (MSA). To be an agurb, a town has to have experienced growth in population or employment from 1990 to 2000 and have per-capita income growing at more than 2 percent per year from 1989 to 1999. Not all small towns are prospering—and therefore not all are classified as agurbs.

Agurban is a continuation of the terms urban and suburban. The first wave of migration within the United States was from the small towns and farms to the urban areas; the second wave was from the urban areas to the suburbs. The third wave—which we are experiencing now, and which constitutes a central theme in this book—is from the suburbs to the agurbs. (See Chapter 2 for discussion of this third wave.)

What you learn about the strengths of these agurbs might surprise you. And it might invigorate your own community.

The Dilemma and the Opportunities

B ig cities hum with vibrancy, as they declare themselves distinct through their commerce and art, their culture and resources, their landmarks and heritage, their climate and geography, their corporate identity. It is no different with small towns. How a town plans, builds, attracts new businesses and determines its community identity all work to create the town's own hum and buzz, its own vibrancy, its own voltage and current.

Small towns have something that suburbs and big cities cannot possess, by nature of their size: In a small town, a person has a greater chance of truly making a difference. Individual success in a small town can spill over into the whole town's success. A person begins a small publishing company, backed by a locally owned bank that is keenly interested in investing in its own community, and that company takes off, employing first five, then 10, then 50, then 100 employees. Along the way, new businesses spring up: a print shop, a software company that partners with the publisher, a video production company that does the same. A graphics design company takes root as well. Freelance writers, editors, photographers, artists and designers find work. The town flourishes.

And this is looking at just one sector of the town; the waves of prosperity overlap into other sectors as well. People in small communities are more directly affected by others' success in their community. The ripple effect can reach to the ends of a town, and the ripples—like the tides of a sea—go both ways. That is, individual success impacts community success, and community success impacts individual success. This happens to a degree in suburbs and cities, but not nearly to the extent it does in small towns.

The opportunities for rural communities to prosper are abundant; the landscape for success in small towns is as fertile as the fields that grace America's heartland. But that success doesn't occur by happenstance. The town that understands the factors that influence its chances of success, and knows the value of having a vision for economic development, will prosper.

Singing a Different Song

Imagine sitting among a group of music experts 30 years ago, trying to decide the best place to locate the premier, live, national music center. These "experts"—all of whom lived in large cities—would make their cases for Nashville, Chicago, Los Angeles, New York, New Orleans or some other major metropolis. They wouldn't have seen the rationale in choosing a little town out in the middle of nowhere—Branson, Missouri, for example.

Branson, after all, was a real nowheresville. It boasted only one small pole-barn theater, Jim Owen's Hillbilly Theater. Owen invited movie stars and singers to pose in front of his theater for pictures, and the local chamber of commerce assisted by promoting Branson's attributes to each of these guests. The townsfolk of Branson didn't know they didn't have a chance of becoming a big center for live music. In fact, they didn't care. They just kept promoting their town, built a second theater and then a third, and kept building until they had more than 30 theaters by 2003. Beginning with one person's vision and passion, a town was transformed, jobs were created, and Branson—with a population of 6,050—became the live music capital of the world. It now attracts more than 7 million visitors annually and boasts more theater seats than Broadway.

Contrast the Branson story with the mythical town of Hayseedville. The town's economy was depressed, and so were the people. They simply didn't see anything redeeming about their community. The town leaders met to discuss their plight, bemoaning the fact that more than half of their high school graduates moved out of the area because of the lack of job opportunities. The leaders wrung their hands in desperation and talked long into the night about all the insurmountable problems they faced. They were poorly located, or they had a less-than-desirable climate, or the interstate was 15 miles away, or a neighboring town had more to offer (and with an outlook like this, it's not hard to see why). The excuses went on and on. Everyone agreed on the woes—the telling of which left them without any energy to venture into possible solutions.

What did the people of Branson see that the people of Hayseedsville didn't? In a word, opportunity.

By the Numbers

The U.S. Census Bureau defines a Metropolitan Statistical Area (MSA) as having at least one city that exceeds 50,000 in population or as an urbanized area (of at least 50,000 inhabitants) with a total metropolitan population of at least 100,000. The 822 MSA counties in the United States showed a 17.9 percent growth in population from 1990 to 2000; the 2,320 non-MSA counties lagged behind at 11.3 percent. More startling, more than half of the 15,800 small towns in America lost population. Most futurists predict this trend will continue well into the 21st century.

The MSA counties topped the smaller counties in two other vital areas: average employment change (14.7 percent for MSAs, 13.1 percent for non-MSAs) and average per-capita income change (50 percent for MSAs, 48.3 percent for non-MSAs).

These figures do not paint a pretty picture for small-town America. Yet residents in small towns still need to make a living. They still need to support their families, pay their bills, put their kids through college, tuck a little money away for retirement and maybe have a few extra dollars to eat at the restaurant down the street. The dilemma for residents in small towns is choosing which company to court to move to the town and figuring out how to keep the local brain trust from moving away. It is in deciding what businesses to invest in; it is in gaining for itself a community identity that attracts tourists and new business, and keeps money flowing in its coffers. It is in keeping its head above water when the flood is overtaking so many small towns around it. Dozens of towns have suffered serious, disabling setbacks, only to rebound from those setbacks and essentially reinvent themselves—coming back stronger than before.

There's a charm to small-town living. Even more, there is an ingenuity in some small towns, an attitude and approach to problem solving, a vision and a work ethic that all work together to pump new life into a place that's barely a speck on a map—but is astoundingly vibrant and healthy within its borders.

The Blond and the Grad Student

Imagine the year is 1949. A beautiful blonde strolls into a Princeton campus bar with four attractive female friends. They see a group of four male grad students—John Nash among them—and the blonde smiles seductively at Nash. The guys ruefully award Nash the "victory"; it is apparent the blonde has chosen him.

But Nash—in the movie *A Beautiful Mind*, at least—uses the moment to crystallize a theory of his. "Now, we could all be selfish," he says to his envious cohorts, "and all go for the blonde. What happens? We end up fighting each other, she walks away and her friends walk out with her. Which means we all lose." The others nod rather grimly at this prospect, for the blonde is beautiful indeed. "Now, what if we were to stop thinking of our own personal gain for a moment, and consider the collective good of the group?" he adds. "What if we were to ignore the blonde and go instead for her four friends?"

Nash's chums ponder this alternative; clearly, the other young women are quite attractive as well, if not as beautiful as the blonde. "That way we each end up with someone beautiful," Nash concludes, "and everyone wins—except for the blonde, who assumed we would fight over her."

In 1994 Nash won the Nobel Prize in Economics for this notion of equilibrium in the case of multiple "players" who are rivals but also share common interests. He took what had traditionally been viewed as a win-lose situation and opened up the possibilities to a win-win situation. This theory, which he posited in 1950, applies not just to social situations but also to business, economics, sports, politics, law and many other fields. Its scope is as global and far-reaching as international relations, and as personal and pointed as individual development and success.

And it directly affects your economic health and the prosperity of the town you live in.

In the traditional win-lose situation, one entity—a person, a company, an organization or a country—vanquishes the opponent, winner take all. The Nash Equilibrium theory allows for multiple winners; rivals can coexist and even mutually benefit one another. Nash's win-win strategy is crucial to the survival of small towns, and it has great implications on the success of the people in those communities. In fact, the win-win solution is played out daily in successful small towns across America.

This is not to say that *all* small towns are economically healthy—or, as Garrison Keillor, the humorist, might put it, places "where all the women are strong, all the men are good-looking and all the children are above average." The stark reality is that small towns are in a fight for survival and, regardless of any theory posed by a Nobel Prize winner, most are losing the fight.

The Solution

A town consists of individuals as well as groups; private citizens and public officials; employers and employees; and a variety of organizations, businesses, groups and other entities. Restaurants, gas stations, clothing stores and other businesses compete against one another for their piece of the town pie. As a business owner, one approach is to undercut your competition, driving prices so low that the consumer wins. But this is repeating the win-lose scenario; in this case, you ultimately lose as your profits go down. While no consumer would argue that prices should be higher, the effect of such an approach is that the town pie, over time, becomes smaller.

As John Nash's theory suggests, there is another approach. The trick is to expand the size of the pie. Everyone wins when the pie becomes larger; everyone has a chance for a bigger piece. Cooperation among "friendly rivals" within a town can result in greater benefits for all town residents.

When businesses, interest groups, and private citizens all work for the common good of the town, the town as a whole has a greater chance to prosper. Think of it this way: Big picture equals big pie. Keeping the big picture in mind—the welfare of the entire town—steers you and your town toward that bigger pie.

Nash had a theory that, in its simplest terms, shined a light on the cooperative strategies among competitors that result in a win-win situation for all involved. This book is rooted in the Nash Equilibrium theory, which can be played out in real lives and real towns and help communities—and the people within them—realize some of their hopes and dreams.

The keys to success are not complex or mysterious. Rather, they are grounded in common sense and tried principle. What's most startling about them is that they are not more commonly adhered to.

These keys are the secrets to success for you as an individual, for your company if you are a business owner, and for your town as a whole.

Back to the Agurbs

L ands' End got its start in 1963, in a basement along the river in Chicago's old tannery district. The company was started by a couple of sailors who made and sold various items for the sailboat crowd.

Although the company grew and prospered in Chicago, it really started to take off in the late 1970s when the company relocated to the rural town of Dodgeville, Wisconsin. Gary Comer, one of the founders and the chairman of the company, moved the business there because he fell in love with its picturesque setting of gently rolling hills, woods and cornfields.

But, according to the company's Web site (landsend.com), Comer discovered something else about the rural setting that was more important for the success of the company: "Along with all that nature had to offer us, we came to know what a remarkable group of people we were joining with in the community," said Comer. "It's a farm community, and our fellow workers were the sons and daughters of farmers and their families included a fine bunch of kids. We quickly found that they are the kind of people who get up mighty early in the morning, because they may have a cow or two to milk before coming to work." The company has found the southern Wisconsin workforce so beneficial that it opened additional operations in neighboring towns after outgrowing the size of Dodgeville's workforce.

Marilyn and Tom Ross, authors of *Country Bound: Trade Your Business Suit Blues for Blue Jean Dreams*, (Communication Creativity, 1997) did just what their book title suggests. They moved from the hustle and bustle of San Diego to the charm and tranquility of Buena Vista, Colorado. In their book, they reveal why they—along with a great number of other big-city dwellers—have made the move to a small town: "Tired of trendiness and materialism, Americans are rediscovering the joys of home life, basic values and roots. They're rediscovering sentimental movies. Mixed-breed dogs. Pot roast. Family reunions....They're connecting with Higher Power. They realize it's time to enjoy the little things, for one day we may realize they were the big things."

You might never have heard of David Gershenson, but how about Terry Bradshaw? As the quarterback for the Pittsburgh Steelers, Terry Bradshaw led his team to four Super Bowl titles from 1975 to 1980; he now co-hosts National Football League pre-game shows. Gershenson manages Terry Bradshaw. And he does it from Silver City, New Mexico.

You would think that Gershenson's job would require him to live in New York, Chicago or Los Angeles. In fact, Gershenson is a Los Angeles native who never envisioned living anywhere else. However, when his ex-wife and their two children moved to Silver City to be closer to her family, Gershenson followed. Speaking of Silver City, Gershenson says, "The quality of life one gets from a community this size is something a person can't put a price tag on." While Gershenson still commutes regularly to Los Angeles, the latest in telecommunications, including video conferencing, allows him to "thrive, not simply survive, the rigors of the rat race. Silver City allows me the space to be a father and keep my priorities straight," he says.

Thurston Williams and Annelle Durham left the hustle and bustle of San Francisco and moved to a 20-acre organic farm in Upper Lake, California. Although they had worked in education and healthcare, Williams said, "Going into farming was a long-term attraction for me. I wanted to do something else before I retired from teaching." They now grow vegetables and grapes and tend plum and apple trees. "The greatest thing besides our love that we ever gave our kids was that we gave them the opportunity of being raised on a farm," Williams said.

Wanda Urbanska and her husband Frank Levering moved from Los Angeles to Orchard Gap, North Carolina, just 12 miles from Mount Airy, actor Andy Griffith's hometown and the fictional site for TV's Mayberry. She was a journalist for the *Los Angeles Herald Examiner*; he wrote screenplays. They have continued writing and have collaborated on two books about their experiences: *Moving to a Small Town: A Guidebook for Moving from Urban to Rural America* (Simon & Schuster, 1996), and *Simple Living: One Couple's Search for a Better Life* (Penguin Books, 1993).

Urbanska writes, "Ours was a fairly common workaholic story that we're seeing in America today. I think it's very easy to get caught up in material acquisition and financial advancement in a big city because that's so much a part of the culture around you. Here, longstanding relationships count for an awful lot. If you know people, you're less concerned about what car they drive, how big their house is, etc. If you get involved in community life, those things start to fade away."

Making the Move

Gary Comer, the Rosses and the others mentioned above are just eight of hundreds of thousands of people who have moved their businesses, their families and their lives to the agurbs.

In fact, according to Dreamtowns.com, more than 18 million people moved from metropolitan areas into small cities or rural counties during the 1990s. The bottom line can be summed up in three words: quality of life. That quality is reflected in a number of ways: lower costs of housing and living, lower crime rates, better schools, shorter commutes and, in general, a more relaxed and less stressful lifestyle. And in terms of operating a business, the costs are much lower in agurbs than in cities. (See Appendix A for lists of the country's top 100 agurbs, as well as all 397 small towns that meet the criteria for an agurb.)

Table 2.1 shows just how healthy the counties of those agurbs are in comparison to all urban counties and to the entire country. (All of the data are compared on a county-wide basis, because no town is an island unto itself. Analyzing the entire county provides a better overall picture.) The percentages refer to increases in employment and population from 1990 to 2000 and increases in per-capita income (PCI) from 1989 to 1999. (For additional agurb-to-city comparisons, see Chapter 12.)

People all across America are discovering that small towns can be a great place to live, raise a family, locate a company, and invest in the future. Agurbs are fast becoming America's worst-kept secret. They are the wave of the future—and for millions of people and hundreds of companies, that wave has already begun.

Table 2.1: Agurb Growth v. City Growth

	Employment Increase	Population Increase	Per-Capita Income Increase
Top 100 Agurbs	32.1%	27.9%	51.1%
All 397 Agurbs	24.0%	19.7%	51.0%
All Urban Counties	14.7%	17.9%	50.0%
All U.S.	13.8%	13.1%	50.0%

Back to the Future

The current move to the agurbs is the third great population wave in the United States' history. Interestingly, the waves represent a complete cycle, with people returning from whence they came—rural areas. The first wave was from farms to urban areas; the second wave, which continues today, is from urban areas to the suburbs; and the third wave is from the suburbs to the agurbs.

The first wave of migration, from the farms to the cities, began in the early 1800s as new technology spurred city growth. From 1800 to 1900, Americans living in cities jumped from less than 20 percent to more than 50 percent of the population. The Industrial Revolution gave birth to many new industries, and factories sprang up to produce the materials and products that supported these industries. It also called for a relatively cheap source of labor to operate the factories and plants. Agrarian workers flocked from the farms to the factories, eager to find a new, better and perhaps easier, way of living. (Farming can be described in many ways, none of which would be "easy.") The lifestyles of poor farmers and field laborers—and of immigrants who came to America for a better life—improved as the nation's industrial output dramatically increased.

But as the cities grew, the quality of life within them began to decrease. No longer were cities the idyllic places in which to raise a family or even to grow a business. Higher rates of crime and higher costs of living—and of operating businesses—took the glow off city life for many. This realization, along with the advent of new technology, eventually led to the second wave of migration within the United States, from the urban areas to the suburbs.

With the arrival of the automobile and the telephone, people had more freedom and flexibility in how they lived their lives, where they lived and where they worked. They no longer had to be able to either walk to work or to a commuter rail line. They could live in a lower cost environment and drive much greater distances to work. This movement from the cities to the suburbs began gathering steam in the 1950s and continues today; it has been in full force since the 1960s. By 1970 the population of the nation's suburbs outranked city populations. This continuing shift to the suburbs has been joined by a third wave: a move to the agurbs.

Technological advances in the last half of the 20th century, especially in the last 20 years or so, have made possible and accelerated the move to agurban areas. Among Fortune 500 companies in 2002 that were headquartered in agurbs were Lowe's (Wilkesboro, North Carolina), Corning (Corning, New York), Cummins (Columbus, Indiana), Maytag (Newton, Iowa), Mohawk Industries (Calhoun, Georgia) and Cooper Tire & Rubber (Findlay, Ohio). Other U.S. corporations have contributed to this shift by showing a growing preference to locate in smaller towns with smaller corporate staffs while giving more autonomy to their regional manufacturing and distribution facilities. In fact, from 1960 to 1990, two-thirds of Fortune 500 companies headquartered in New York City left for greener pastures.

As a country, America is returning to its rural roots—but armed with powerful technological tools that have shrunk the world so one can live a high-quality life and operate a successful business "out in the boondocks." Unlike the first wave of migration, which mainly involved unskilled laborers, this third wave is primarily undertaken by skilled and educated people who

Whistling While You Work—At Home

Paul Horberg, a client representative for IBM, telecommutes 150 miles each day. "I've been doing it for about seven years," he says. "Being in the office isn't as important as it was in the beginning. We have a program within IBM that acts like an Instant Messenger program. One person can pose a question to several hundred others and have an answer in minutes. This is probably more efficient than being in the office."

Chris Hansen, director of information services for the State Universities Retirement System of Illinois, covers the entire state with pension counselors for the almost 150,000 members scattered throughout the state. Several years ago, Hansen began working with counselors away from the main office in Champaign.

"Using telecom facilities to connect remote locations has been an option since I started in the business in the early '70s, but its use was limited because of price and speed. Over time price has been decreasing while both hardware and software have gotten faster," Hansen says. "We started off with dedicated lines at a cost of $1,500 to $2,000 per month, went to ISDN lines at a cost of $1,000 per month, and now are using DSL technology at a cost of less than $100 per month. In the future we'll see satellite and wireless technology being widely used at even lower costs.

"I've got several friends and associates who are telecommuting every day," Hansen continues. "They are project managers, medical transcribers, marketing managers and even an attorney."

choose to live not only outside a city but also outside its sprawling suburbs. Many people are realizing that they can, if they so desire, move to the agurbs and continue to do their work while further enhancing their quality of life.

Today, computer technology, laptops, the Internet, e-mail, mobile phones, videoconferencing and an array of other technologies have opened the door for corporate America to operate in vastly different ways than it did only 20 years ago. Telecommuting is on the rise; employers find it cost-effective to allow many employees to work from distant locations, with no impediments to productivity. In fact, from 1999 to 2001, the number of Americans who telework (work exclusively from home, at telework centers, at satellite offices, on the road or some combination of these) rose from 19.6 million to 28 million, according to the International Telework Association and Council. The small towns that invest in the infrastructure to support telecommuting, such as broadband connectivity, can tap into this trend.

Jobs are outsourced; consultants and freelancers are hired on a per-project basis, without the employer taking on the burden of full-time employment, including insurance and healthcare costs. And not only do some employees relocate to agurbs and telecommute but also new factories and plants—more streamlined and focused—are going up in small towns. The companies that build these factories are taking advantage of improvements in transportation and shipping cost and time, and in overall operating costs that small towns can offer.

It's a win-win situation made possible by technology, and it is changing the face of corporate America today. Those changes will continue long into the future.

The Tales of Two One-Horse Towns

All this good news, however, only opens the door to opportunity; it doesn't guarantee success for the people who move to small towns or for the towns themselves. As Will Rogers, the humorist, once said, "Even if you're on the right track, you'll get run over if you just sit there."

We all know people who have stayed with the same company even though they didn't like their employer and didn't make much money. They stayed out of fear; they held on tight and didn't let go. And we know people who may have moved from company to company, but always in the same position—they made lateral moves and never attempted to move up, again out of fear or lack of confidence. They, too, were holding on tight, not letting go of their image of themselves and their capabilities. And they were being left behind in the process.

What Others Are Saying

Broadband and Wi-Fi are among the technological developments that make it possible for virtually every town and city to be on equal footing in terms of communications. Add the development of small, affordable business jets, which form a nationwide air-taxi service at the cost of a business-class ticket, and you have all of the advantages of being located in a major hub city. But you do so at the lower cost and higher quality of life benefits.

Dorrene Benthin of GVNW Consulting, a national telecommunications consulting firm located in Tualatin, Oregon, spoke of the need to get the rural message out: "Some businesses still think rural areas communicate by carrier pigeon. But these communities can offer broadband, high-speed access, digital connectivity—it's all there. But we have to get the message out. Rural communities have lots of low-cost land. And their people are generally very eager to help a new company settle in. They're excited about new jobs that will stem the great out-migrations of their young people looking for jobs."

Several futurists have written extensively about this trend, including Harry S. Dent, author of *The Roaring 2000s* (Touchstone, 1998). In that book, Dent writes that most people aren't living smarter by moving their homes and work to big cities and suburbs, which have higher costs of living and a decreasing quality of life. Over the next 30 years, Dent expects to see at least 70 million people escape the overcrowded and increasingly expensive suburbs. Where will they go? He thinks the most attractive locations will be smaller towns, new growth cities, 'exurban' areas, and even back to older 'hip' urban areas.

In 2002, Rich Karlgaard, publisher of *Forbes*, wrote a series of articles about the resurgence of rural America. In one issue of *Forbes* (April 15, 2002), Karlgaard refers to his theory as The Boonyack Comeback: "Small U.S. cities could very well outperform larger cities economically over the next decade. Small cities, especially towns in warm climates with nearby universities strong in science and engineering, may turn out to be the rising stars of the early 2000s."

The same thing can happen to towns. Consider Bartlesville, Oklahoma (population 34,568). Since 1917 Bartlesville has been home to the Phillips Petroleum Company, and the town prospered through the years. The company poured money into the community, pumping new life into its civic center and making sizeable donations to charity. The townspeople felt a part of the Phillips Petroleum family.

In 2001, Phillips announced a merger with Conoco Inc., to create the world's sixth-largest oil and gas company. The new company, ConocoPhillips, is headquartered in Houston, Texas. While Phillips assured the town that it would still maintain a "significant presence"—which meant keeping information technology, finance, human resources, research and development and several support services in Bartlesville—the message was that Bartlesville would have to reinvent itself. Granted, warning signs had been evident for years: Phillips went from employing 9,100 in Bartlesville in 1981, to 3,200 in 1995, to 2,400 in 2001. Even though Bartlesville was not caught off guard, how the town rebounds will depend greatly on its ability to attract new companies.

Such a rebound is far from unheard of. Thomaston, Georgia, home to Thomaston Mills, is a perfect example of a one-company town. The textile mill, which wove fabrics and the cotton from nearby cotton fields, employed virtually all of the labor force in Thomaston (population 9,400). The picturesque small town boomed during the textile explosion in the South during the 20th century. However, cheaper imports from overseas began to erode this industry during the 1990s. On June 14, 2001, word came that Thomaston Mills, still locally owned and managed, would shut its doors for good. Suddenly, 2.5 million square feet of space was on the market and at least 1,400 people were without jobs.

Thomaston neither panicked nor succumbed. Betsy Hueber, president of the Thomaston-Upson Chamber of Commerce, recalls, "Within three days the local chamber of commerce brought together city and state officials to develop a plan of action. Within days the group developed plans to address two main issues: one, human issues of unemployment, and two, community development—how to recruit in new industry to fill 2.5 million square feet of space, much of which was obsolete."

Working together with a number of governmental sources, the group offered new job training to many unemployed people, with special 52-week unemployment benefits if they continued their schooling. Several smaller textile mills bought pieces of the former Thomaston Mills and hired local residents.

The state, working with local officials, drew new industries into the town. New trades sprouted. The town turned disaster into opportunity.

The unemployment rate in Thomaston exceeded 15 percent in 2001, but that was cut in half in a little over a year. The community is back on its feet after the shock of the local icon's closing, building an 80,000-square-foot spec building and buying more land to expand an industrial park. Thomaston's goal is to continue to diversify its base, recruiting more firms like Quad-Graphics, which employs 600 in the printing industry; Yamaha Music, with 300 employees; and Duni Plastics, with 150 employees.

Unlike Thomaston, many towns in need of changing their futures and their fortunes by reexamining their visions and economic development plans often stand pat, grim and determined, resistant to any change. The civic leaders and residents in these towns are "willing to go down with the ship"—and quite often that's exactly what happens. Often, these people develop an attitude of "we sure showed them," especially when they have refused to work out something with a large employer and the company subsequently leaves town. Little do they realize that the company will quickly move on while the town's workforce is often stuck in a rut of lower-paying, less-fulfilling jobs.

The "good old days" can take you only so far. The towns that survive hits like Thomaston took, the towns that thrive in today's fast-paced, ever-changing world, have visions for themselves, are forward-thinking, are willing to change and indeed are *looking* to change—or to continue to grow.

Five Factors Favoring Prosperity

The relationship between town and individual prosperity is reciprocal. You can measure success in small towns by growth in population, in jobs and in per-capita income. Although there are other definitions and measurements of success, these three are quantifiable, clear indicators of a town's economic health and growth.

There is no one road to success, just as there are no two small towns that are exactly alike (and if you think otherwise, just suggest so to a small-town resident—and prepare yourself for battle, because you have just thrown down the gauntlet). However, five societal trends and factors have opened the doors to small-town growth; typically, a thriving town understands and takes advantage of the following factors:

1. Forces of Freedom. A number of shifts—some occurring 20 or more years ago and some in the aftermath of the terrorist attacks on September 11, 2001— have shaped the way America does business within its borders and around the world. Deregulation of several industries—airlines, telecommunications and trucking chief among them—has resulted in lower prices for consumers and increased profits for those companies flexible enough to compete in a new environment as government has loosened its control. Deregulation has allowed industries to grow closer to the customers and respond better to their needs.

The Staggers Act: Derailing Regulation

From 1897 to 1980, railroads were among the most regulated industries in the United States. Rates; services; car utilization; and the construction, sales, and closures of rail lines were all subject to strict economic regulation. The cumbersome regulations reflected the fact that railroads, at one time, had a transportation monopoly in the United States. However, the rail share of the freight transportation market dropped to 35 percent in the late 1970s. Trucks, barges, Great Lakes carriers, pipelines and planes had captured the rest.

When Congress passed the Staggers Rail Act of 1980, railroads, trucking and airlines were permitted to operate more like other businesses. Named for Rep. Harley O. Staggers, chairman of the House Commerce Committee, the Staggers Act ushered in new life for the entire transportation industry—one that has attracted new business, reduced costs, increased service and safety and stimulated new investment in what, before 1980, was a weak industry.

As a result of deregulation, logistics costs represented 8.7 percent of the U.S. Gross Domestic Product in 2002. This is down from 9.5 percent in 2001 and down from 16.2 percent in 1981, the first full year of interstate trucking deregulation.

Roger Roberson's family trucking company in Farmer City, Illinois, was one of the hundreds that benefited from the deregulation that followed passage of the legislation. Over the previous 10 years the company had filed applications for almost 2,000 different operating authorities for each route and each commodity it wanted to carry. Deregulation enabled Roberson's company to compete with much larger trucking firms on an equal footing. Within four years of deregulation, Roberson had doubled the size of his firm from $28 million to $56 million and has continued growing to more than $100 million in sales annually. Today his company is one of the top 100 trucking firms in the United States.

As an example, Southwest Airlines began in the early 1970s as a small airline flying between Dallas, Houston and San Antonio, Texas. Deregulation allowed Southwest to expand its low-cost, focused strategy throughout the United States. Southwest has helped to make air travel less expensive for consumers, and the stock market has rewarded Southwest with a market cap for its stock *twice* all of the other U.S. airlines.

Globalization and the global economy suffered a severe—but not unprecedented—setback after September 11, 2001. A similar global setback occurred in the 1930s, brought on first by the Great Depression and then World War II. In times of war (and now, with increased diligence in guarding against future terrorist attacks), borders tighten, international trade slows, cross-border transportation and shipping prices and insurance rise, and the poor—whether in terms of people, companies, or countries—get pinched as trade tightens.

Globalization and free trade have transformed industry after industry, as international competition undercuts once-mighty American conglomerates and corporations. One giant brought to bankruptcy is Bethlehem Steel, which in the 1960s produced more than 8,000 tons of molten iron a day. Bethlehem, with its massive machine shops, was beaten by smaller overseas companies and new U. S. competitors that used more effective means and new technologies to produce steel.

Bethlehem Steel is not alone in its demise. Although U.S. demand for steel continues to grow at about 40 percent each year, American steel companies have lost nearly 350,000 jobs since 1979. At least 27 steel companies have filed for bankruptcy since 1998. The old steel giants are being replaced by a new breed of smaller, quicker, more efficient steel makers—22 percent of which are located on foreign soil.

The clear losers in globalization are companies that are huge, cumbersome, and weighted down with backward thinking—companies that have inflated labor costs and are slow to take advantage of new technologies that lead to greater efficiency and productivity. The winners are willing to adapt, downsize, embrace new technologies that can increase their productivity and service, and find ways to keep operating costs low while expanding their markets. Globalization is a direct product of democracy and freedom, and it brings out the best for the consumer.

What does this have to do with small towns? Plenty. More and more corporations and industries that have traditionally been entrenched in major metropolitan areas are seeing the benefits of moving plants and operations to rural—and formerly "small market"—locales. With today's technology, lines between small and big markets have become blurred or have vanished altogether. Small towns stand to benefit from the forces of freedom that have shaped, and will continue to influence, the economy both at home and abroad.

2. Ready and Willing Labor. Companies like what they see in rural and small-town labor forces. In fact, the rural workforce is a primary reason that companies are packing up and heading out to the country. Dr. John C. Allen, an associate professor of rural sociology at the University of Nebraska-Lincoln, told Lisa A. Bastian (writing for *Area Development Online*) that rural people are known for "their morals, especially in terms of being responsible; their view of their work as careers, not jobs; and their willingness to work not just to collect a paycheck, but to help the employer achieve success." According to Allen, only three percent of rural Nebraskans plan on moving, and quite often they go out of their way to be able to stay in their community.

Randall Shedd, director of Cullman County Economic Development in Alabama, knows the power of ready and willing labor. "We found that our strong agriculture-based economy was an asset in our industrial recruiting efforts," Shedd says. "Sam Walton [Wal-Mart founder] said when he flew over Cullman County and saw all the chicken houses, it reminded him of home and he knew the people of Cullman County would work. He said that was one of the primary reasons he chose Cullman County for one of his 1-million-square-foot distribution centers."

Small towns traditionally are inhabited by people with strong work ethics, partly because so many of them grew up on farms. A farm day is long: The work is never finished, and the labor is physical and hard. Farmers learn the four P's: patience, perseverance, persistence and, perhaps most important, perpetuity. They work hard, go to bed, and get up early the next morning to do it all over again. Asking someone with this work ethic to put in eight hours a day in a factory, mill, plant, warehouse, distribution center or office center is nothing. As one laborer in rural Utah commented after a company had recently hired him and then told him to take off Labor Day, "You mean I get to take the day off and I get paid for doing it?"

You'll find the same work ethic in those who have never lived on a farm but have lived in small towns their whole lives. People in small towns tend to be more invested in their community and in their jobs; people in cities, on the other hand, trade deep roots for greater mobility. Companies recognize this and are increasingly willing to move to rural communities to find a hard-working, reliable labor force.

Not too many years ago in this country, people were on the go, moving from city to city and job to job—following the money—while companies were content to be sought out. Now, the roles are reversed, at least in rural communities: It's the *companies* that are looking to relocate to smaller (and more cost-effective) locales, while rural residents are content to stay put. They no longer need to follow the money because the money is following them.

3. Lowered Costs. Operating a business in a rural setting, by and large, costs much less than in a city. In 2000, Iogistics, Inc., a consulting firm that helps companies focus on efficiency and cost savings, conducted a study that compared relative costs of distributing products throughout the United States. The study found significant cost savings in land acquisition, labor, labor productivity and housing when comparing small towns to mid-sized cities such as Indianapolis and Memphis. For a company making 50,000 shipments a day, such as a Lands' End or an L.L. Bean, this savings amounts to $5 to $38 million annually, depending upon the location.

4. Improved Communications and Travel. The ease and costs of communicating and traveling have dramatically improved over the past century. According to the World Bank, the transport and communication costs of today, compared to those same costs in 1920, are far lower: Ocean freight costs about 30 percent of what it did in 1920, and air transport costs about 18 percent of its 1920 costs. A similar comparison for transatlantic phone calls (about one percent) is even more impressive.

Traditionally, cities have been strategically located at the axis of communication and travel links: by a railroad junction, by a port, on a river. Big business would locate, naturally enough, in big cities, taking advantage of a larger workforce and easier access to transporting goods. But with today's sophisticated communications networks, this logic no longer holds true. The lines between home and work have blurred as more people telework. Use of the Internet provides a good example of how people have changed their way of doing business. In 1990, the Internet was virtually unknown, except to a handful of academics. By 1997, about 57 million people had tapped into it (71 million, if you include people who use it only for e-mail). In the spring of 2002, *Business Week* estimated that more than 500 million people use the Internet. The numbers continue to increase exponentially; in the not-so-distant future, the gap between Internet users and phone users (the current world stock of phones is 700 million) will continue to narrow until it disappears.

Through Internet networking, companies can reach customers with unprecedented ease and efficiency. Shopping, purchases, product tracking, invoicing and an expanse of other information can all be available to suppliers, distributors and customers via the Internet. This is good news for small towns, because it breaks down the walls that kept them from big business before information technology changed the face of American commerce.

Another boon to small towns is the advent of new airplane technology. Soon the cost of smaller jet airplanes will fall under $2 million, making it quicker and cheaper to fly short distances (with much of the flight scheduling being done over the Internet). NASA conducted a time-and-motion study in the late 1990s and found that the majority of air journeys included trips of 500 miles or less and that traveling by commercial airline was no faster than driving a car. Today's hub-and-spoke airlines system—the United States has 31 hubs and 700 spokes—is not conducive to travel under 500 miles. Door-to-door car travel is nearly as fast as flying, according to the NASA study. But the jetliners of the future will be able to zip travelers from one small airport to another, avoiding the hubs altogether—and at lower prices. More than 5,000 small airports currently handle about 37 million takeoffs and landings annually, but NASA estimates those airports could accommodate 500 million takeoffs and landings.

Another advantage of smaller planes is their flexibility: Commercial jets can fly into 580 airports across the country while private aircraft can fly directly into 5,400 airports. Currently, more than 80 percent of U.S. air travel is conducted from the busiest one percent of airports, and this air travel has become increasingly frustrating, as the nation's big carriers have reduced the number of cities they fly into (from 463 in 1978 to 268 in the late 1990s). Consider the fact that 98 percent of Americans live within a 30-minute drive from one of the more than 5,000 smaller airports, and you see the incentive to move toward the new, smaller jets.

Graph 2.1: Acres Per Person

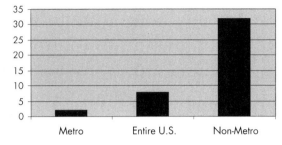

5. **Quality of Life.** This factor is difficult to quantify, but it is also hard to deny that the idyllic life of small towns acts as a magnet for people and businesses alike. The mix is simple: Begin with hardworking people who care about their neighbors and their towns; add in lower costs of living and the advances of technology that remove any barriers to doing business in a small town; consider the cleaner environment and quicker access to natural resources such as lakes, mountains, woods and rivers; and factor in shorter work commutes and lower crime rates.

Part of the allure of small towns is *space*. Some people feel suffocated in a big city, with its massive buildings and large populations. Going to the country affords them not only a breath of fresh air but also a place to stretch without bumping into someone else. The average population per square mile of land in the United States, rounded off to the nearest whole number, is 80 for the entire country, 320 for all metropolitan areas, and 20 for non-metropolitan areas. Or, as shown in graph 2.1, the number of acres per person equals two for the metro area, eight for the entire United States, and 32 for the non-metro area.

Another attribute of small towns is the belief among residents that they can make a difference within their community. This leads to a vitality and shared interest that just aren't as evident in larger cities, as these examples illustrate:

- July 6, 1994, started off as just another day in Glenwood Springs, Colorado, a picturesque mountain community noted for its natural springs and several grand hotels built in the late 1800s. When lightning struck seven miles west of the town, it ignited a fire that quickly took on a life of its own. In mid-afternoon a combination of fuel, terrain and wind changed the fire into a raging inferno, and the hillside exploded in a mass of flame and smoke. A dozen firefighters and several others did not survive—the worst loss of life in a forest fire since the 1950s. Glenwood Springs quickly came to the aid of the victims' families, raising funds and holding memorial services. A Storm King Trail Memorial now honors the 14 men and women who gave their lives to protect the town.

- Although no one perished, 58 people lost their jobs on March 20, 2002, when a restaurant burned down in Nevada City, California. Within days the other local bars and restaurants established a day when a percentage of sales and tips were collected for those 58 employees. In the following month, 30 area musicians donated their time for a local benefit concert. In all, more than $50,000 was raised to help those who lost their jobs as a result of the fire.

- In response to the terrorist attacks of 9/11, Jackson County, Indiana, set up a scholarship fund for the children of the citizens and rescue workers who were killed. Jackson County, with only 40,000 residents, raised more than $125,000 for the fund.

7½ Keys to Success

The factors that make it possible for people in small towns to prosper are in place, but small-town success doesn't happen automatically. Far too many small towns are withering on the vine for that to be the case.

There are 7½ keys that successful people in small towns live by. These keys are just as important for people in cities as well, but personal impact on the city is minimal at best; personal impact on a small town can make or break the town.

The keys—which apply to individuals, to companies and to towns themselves—may not be present to the same degree in all prospering small towns, but collectively they make the difference between withering on the vine and being fruitful. They are covered in depth in the chapters that follow.

1. Adopt a Can-Do Attitude
2. Shape Your Vision
3. Leverage Your Resources
4. Raise Up Strong Leaders
5. Encourage an Entrepreneurial Approach
6. Maintain Local Control
7. Build Your Brand
7 ½. Embrace the Teeter-Totter Factor

Investing in Rural America—and Reaping the Rewards

Sam Walton opened his first Wal-Mart in Rogers, Arkansas, in 1962. Kmart, by coincidence, was also started in 1962 (the company had previously been known as S.S. Kresge). Part of Kmart's strategy was to dominate the urban areas—a sound strategy, given the greater population density in those areas. Typically, Kmart wouldn't open a store in a city of less than 50,000, and the retail chain centralized its distribution in, or close to, these same urban markets.

Sam Walton had another theory. People in rural areas bought products from discount retail stores, didn't they? Perhaps more to the point: Costs of operating distribution centers and stores would be lower in rural areas, wouldn't they? Those two questions were rhetorical for Walton; he knew the answers. He located Wal-Mart's corporate offices and opened Wal-Mart's first distribution center in Bentonville, Arkansas (population 5,508), in 1970, and he began planting Wal-Marts in small towns, as well as suburbs and cities. (Thanks in large part to Wal-Mart's expansion, Bentonville grew to 19,730 by 2000; today the town is part of the Fayetteville-Springdale-Rogers MSA.)

Soon, Wal-Mart versus Kmart began to play like David versus Goliath. In 1971, Kmart was 30 times larger than the upstart retailer, and the smart money would have been on the giant to survive any kind of retail battle. After all, Kmart's net profit was much greater than Wal-Mart's total take.

The smart money would have been wrong.

How wrong? If you had invested $1,000 in each company at the time of its Initial Public Offering—Wal-Mart's came in October 1970, Kmart's in April 1976—your investments, as of December 18, 2002, would have yielded about $29 from Kmart and about $6.3 million from Wal-Mart. Why December 18th? That is the day Kmart's stock was delisted from the New York Stock Exchange after the company filed for bankruptcy in January 2002. Since filing for bankruptcy, Kmart—which has kept its distribution centers in metropolitan areas—has closed 610 stores, 80 percent of which were located in metro areas.

Wal-Mart has 90 distribution centers today, 70 of them outside the biggest metro areas. Kmart has 17 distribution centers left, with 12 of them located within the 50 biggest metro areas. Wal-Mart's distribution system is held up as a model for the future. Walton's decision to locate distribution centers and stores in rural areas proved to be the stone in the sling that slew Goliath. And remember your $1,000 of Kmart stock? Once the company emerged from bankruptcy in May, 2003, it was worth zero. Your $1,000 of Wal-Mart stock? As of November 2003, it had grown to $7.2 million.

Key #1: Adopt a Can-Do Attitude

R obert F. Kennedy spoke perfectly to a "Can-Do" attitude: "There are those who look at things the way they are, and ask why....I dream of things that never were and ask why not?"

This nation was built on a can-do attitude. Without it, the American Revolution would not have happened; independence would not have been achieved. People would not have struck it rich in the Great Gold Rush of 1849. Slavery would not have ended, and a man would not have walked on the moon. Thanks to its positive attitude, this country weathered the storms that came with the Great Depression and several world wars to become a world leader. It has witnessed people from all backgrounds pull together as one in times of crisis, such as the 9/11 terrorist attacks on New York City, Washington, D.C., and Pennsylvania. In short, the United States would not be what it is today if its can-do attitude were somehow stripped away.

That attitude emanates from a spirit that gets to the core of who Americans are and what they are about: opportunity and freedom. A can-do attitude flows from people believing in themselves and in their abilities and fearlessly pursuing their hopes, desires and dreams. Countless Americans have realized their dreams, aided by the freedom and democracy of the land of opportunity within which they operate.

Freedom and individualism were the driving forces throughout the land long before the founding fathers put quill to parchment to formalize those tenets in the Declaration of Independence, the U.S. Constitution and the Bill of Rights. Americans believe in themselves and in their dreams because they have been given no reason not to.

Of course, not every American has a can-do attitude. People are far more complex than that; each person is shaped by his or her environment, upbringing and experiences. Not everyone has the same opportunities in life, and not everyone has the same outlook.

In terms of a town's health and progress, it is ideal that certain people—the mayor, the town attorney, the town manager, the chamber of commerce director, the economic developer and members of the town council—all have a can-do attitude that permeates their discussions, agendas and goals. This doesn't mean there won't be disagreements. It means that differing opinions will be aired and disagreements addressed in a spirit of cooperation and with a focus on what's best for the town and how the people involved can collectively achieve that ideal.

It All Begins With Attitude

Cyclist Lance Armstrong won his fifth straight Tour de France bike race in 2003. An astounding feat in itself, Armstrong's achievement is even more remarkable when you consider he was diagnosed with testicular cancer in 1996. Faced with the ultimate do-or-die situation, Armstrong came through, beating first the cancer and then beating the world's best cyclists for five straight years, beginning in 1999.

To say that Armstrong has a can-do attitude is the understatement of the year. Fittingly, the bike he rides is manufactured by Trek Bicycle Corporation, a small privately owned company in the agurb of Waterloo, Wisconsin. In 1976, when Trek began operations in a barn with five employees, no one would have predicted that it would someday pass such companies as Schwinn, Roadmaster or other giants in the bicycle industry. Yet while American bike manufacturers have been battered by foreign competition, Trek has carved out a niche as a high-end, superior quality product and grown into the largest U.S. bike manufacturer.

Trek's history is much like Lance Armstrong's. The company almost went under in the mid-1980s due to poor quality, which alienated many of its dealers. However, just as its most famous rider persevered and overcame tremendous obstacles, Trek fixed its problems, invested in new technology and grew into an industry leader. In each case, attitude played a critical role in persevering against great odds and eventually succeeding.

The same can happen for a town. Consider the story of Leavenworth, Washington.

Nestled in the mountains of the Wenatchee National Forest, Leavenworth was a sawmill and lumber town in the early part of the 20th century. After the Great Northern Railway Company left town, however, the sawmill and logging industry slowly disintegrated. For a few decades, Leavenworth was on the verge of extinction. By the early 1960s, the town's population had dwindled from more than 5,000 to 1,100. Boarded-up buildings filled its downtown. But the town didn't panic.

The Vesta Junior Women's Club, 11 women strong, saw all of the young people leaving town and decided to do something about it. In 1962, they called upon the Bureau of Community Development at the University of Washington and asked for advice on how to turn around the town's fortunes. Mayor Bill Bauer remembers, "They spent a lot of time in the town and came up with lots of ideas. The university people didn't give them the answers. Over two-thirds of the town was involved, and the town ended up answering its own question. They saw hope in tourism. There were two gentlemen who had a Bavarian-themed restaurant near town, and the Bavarian theme idea just started to grow. While the city council was OK with the idea, I'm not sure how enthusiastic they were at the time."

One of those two men, Ted Price, describes the experience in a book titled *Miracle Town* (Price & Rodgers, 1997). Here are some of the responses he recalls hearing from townspeople who attended those early meetings:

"It won't work!"

"Where are you going to get the money for it?"

"You're not an expert—how do you expect to do that without professional know-how?"

"Why can't you leave things the way they are? Why do you have to change things?"

"We don't want any 'furiners' here from Seattle! No outsider is going to tell us what to do!"

"Why a German theme? We don't have a lot of Germans here."

"Tourism isn't an industry—we never made a nickel on a tourist yet!"

"You're just here to make a lot of money off of us!"

Despite those less-than-ringing endorsements, Price and a few others pushed ahead. He and his partner bought six old buildings for a total of $29,350. LaVerne Peterson, one of the original 11 Vesta Junior Women's Club members, risked everything she had to remodel her Chikamin Hotel into the Hotel Edelweiss. By the mid-1960s various groups had refurbished 12 buildings, and in April 1968 *LOOK* magazine designated Leavenworth as its All-American City for "their distinction by that extra spark of honest openness that encourages hometown people to care, to act and to prove that Americans can still live together productively and peacefully."

Mayor Bauer notes, "From that point on we just grew on our own. We did it without any federal or state grants. We pulled money out of our pockets, and the idea of a Bavarian village town just took off. We've added festivals all through the year and bring in over 1.5 million people each year." Looking ahead, the town is remodeling an old fruit warehouse into a community/festival hall for events, has teamed up with the Audubon Society to create a special center for bird watching, and is helping area apple farmers diversify with other crops. For example, several wineries have opened in the area.

Leavenworth today is a vibrant, growing community of 2,074 with a bright future—thanks to a small group of women who wanted to offer something better for the town's young people and to a few people who had the vision to transform the town into something different, armed only with the determination to make the effort succeed.

Half Full or Half Empty?

Leavenworth could have seen its glass as half empty when its railroad and lumber industries soured. After all, the town is not in a heavily populated area, had no other industry to depend upon and had no real hopes of reviving the industries that had supported it historically.

It could easily have become a ghost town—a remnant of a town that didn't make it, one that perished because it couldn't adjust when its economy went south and its residents died or moved. People in ghost towns, or towns that are beginning to die, often don't see any way out. In fact, they are often so preoccupied with their descent down a slippery slope that they don't have time to grab onto a solution.

"The Can Do Poem"

One of my favorite poems, an anonymous one that applies to small towns, is called "The Can Do Poem." Part of it goes this way:

If you think you are beaten, you are
If you think you dare not, you don't
If you'd like to win, but think you can't
It's almost a cinch, you won't
Because life's battles don't always go
To the stronger or faster man
Sooner or later, the person that wins
Is the one who says, I CAN!!

Tell City, Indiana: An Earth-Moving Experience

Tell City is a river town in southern Indiana. Named after William Tell, it was founded by Swiss immigrants in 1858 as a cooperative community and operated as a woodworking manufacturing center. The town, which has about 8,000 residents, is located 25 miles from the nearest interstate. Adding to its old-world charm are wide streets shaded by mature trees, rolling hills, and wooded land that rises above the banks of the Ohio River.

Tell City fell on tough times in the 1980s and early 1990s. The Tell City Chair Company, a furniture manufacturer that employed 1,000 people, closed its doors in 1996; employment at the General Electric plant dropped from 2,000 employees in the 1980s to 105 in 2002. Greg Wathen, director of the economic development group for Perry County, in which Tell City is located, came on board in 1992, bringing a can-do attitude. "If you build it, they will come," Greg says. "If you don't build it, they won't."

Armed with that simple philosophy, a disarmingly cheery outlook and the determination of a bulldog, Wathen set about the task—with the help of many others in the community—of resurrecting Tell City's economy. In 1994, Wathen negotiated the Tell City Port Authority's purchase of 26 miles of track from the Norfolk Southern, which was abandoning the rail line into the town. The first year the renamed Hoosier Southern Railroad shipped only eight railcars. Now more than 2,500 railcars of product per year are shipped to local and regional companies, providing them with a competitive advantage. Locally owned banks set up a $5 million unsecured line of credit to assist the community in its project.

In the mid-1990s, Tell City was a finalist for a major company that liked its central location and proximity to customers. Wathen knew that this project would help revitalize his hometown. However, the rolling topography of the river town didn't lend itself easily to construction of a suitable facility. As the president of the company and Wathen flew from Tell City to Indianapolis one day, the president noted that, while he really liked the town, the obstacle of moving so much dirt to complete the project would be a deal-stopper.

On the spot, without anyone's authorization, Wathen committed to get the job done, and the deal was consummated. Two million cubic feet later, after an investment of both state and local funds, the largest earth-moving project in Indiana's history resulted in construction of a multimillion-dollar facility with 900 jobs paying an average of more than $40,000 per year. Wathen's approach illustrates the can-do attitude that can change a community, transforming it from one that is slowly dying into a vibrant, growing one.

People in towns like Leavenworth have the ability to quell the panic in their stomachs and assess their situation from a different perspective. They take the time to reinvent their town and construct "Plan B," one whose outcome will exceed the original plan. It's not hard for people in any town to see a host of problems when the local economy takes a hit and businesses begin to close or leave. But the Leavenworths of the world see their glass as half full. Even as the moving vans are pulling away, they see new opportunities behind the current challenges.

In small towns, the people who are energized by challenges and thrive on problem solving can influence the whole community; they can pull others along with them. Yet merely being hopeful or positive isn't enough. You need to combine this outlook with a visionary way of thinking and a gritty determination to carry out the new plan that evolves from that thinking. When these qualities are combined, they begin to forge a can-do attitude that is critical to personal and business success, especially in times of trouble.

A can-do attitude is literally a defender; you can wield it as a mighty sword against the onslaught of the enemy. In the case of Leavenworth, the enemy— the flagging economy—appeared ready to strike a lethal blow. But, guided by its spirit and attitude, the town triumphed.

Personality Types

All towns take on an organic quality; they can flourish or fade, bloom or wilt, wax or wane. Towns also take on a personality, a mentality that mimics the people who inhabit them. These personalities can be described in terms of animals:

- **Mules.** Drive into a Mule town and you get the sense that this community is not only opposed to change but also proud of the way it is (and has been for many generations). "What worked for my great-grandfather is good enough for me" is a commonly shared sentiment in Mule communities. Mules take fierce pride in who they are (or were) and what they're about—even if the rest of the world passed them by 50 years ago.

  Sometimes people are so set against change that they close off to all possibilities, even if the change presents good opportunities to the community. Many lumber and railroad towns have shrunk and shriveled because they adamantly refused to change when change was necessary to their health. In such instances it's hollow comfort indeed to know that you "didn't give in, didn't change your ways"—with bitter consequences as a result of that stubborn and willful allegiance to a past that can no longer nurture the present.

- **Moles.** Mole communities don't share the fierce attitude of their Mule compatriots—but they do have the same dismal outlook. Mole communities are always behind the times, never at the forefront, and are often left behind altogether because of their unwillingness to consider change, to be forward thinking, to take appropriate risks, to be bold. They may appreciate a can-do attitude but can't collectively muster enough of it within their town to change their regressive ways. Like Mules, they resist change; but Moles' resistance stems from fear, not obstinacy.

These communities have a fear of failure rather than a thirst for success. A Mole town might have great ideas for bringing in new commerce, but the people can't muster the courage to bring it off. Such towns court businesses but don't make the necessary commitments. They talk about investing in the future, leveraging their resources to greater advantage, and revitalizing their town, but nothing ever happens. Something is always on the *verge* of happening, but the town can't bring itself to take the final steps to make it happen.

As a result, Mole towns are left in the dust of more progressive towns. They look at other towns' successes and wistfully or jealously say, "That could have been us. *We* could have done that." They could have and should have. But they didn't, and they're left to lament the fact. Such towns hold much promise but rarely deliver on that promise.

- **Jackals.** Deep down, Jackal communities are fearful as well, but they respond much differently than Mole communities. Jackals lash out, deriding other communities that take risks and meet new challenges head-on. Jackals prefer to sit back and watch others fail, rather than move forward and try to succeed themselves. Like Mules and Moles, they prefer to stand pat but do so with an attitude—one that definitely isn't a can-do attitude.

Jackal communities are parasitic: They want to live off the success of others even as they deride the risks successful towns take and the attitudes that helped those towns calculate, and then take, those risks in the first place. For example, consider the town that believes in and invests in itself and does quite well as a tourist town—much to the barely disguised disdain of a neighboring town 10 miles down the road. "We'd never compromise ourselves and turn into one more tourist trap," folks from the neighboring town would say. However, they wouldn't turn away the greatly increased motel and restaurant business in *their* town, brought about by the other town's "compromise."

- **Eagles.** Eagle communities possess, among other characteristics, the positive attitude needed to make and keep a town successful. Eagle communities aren't fearful of what others think of them; rather, they focus on what they need and want and how to achieve it.

Satchel Paige, the great baseball pitcher, once said, "Don't look back. Something might be gaining on you." Mules, Moles and Jackals are constantly looking back, but Eagles remain intent on looking *forward*. Eagles have great vision, which helps them get what they want. They also are proud and fearless; they pay no heed to rumors, gossip, petty concerns, "what ifs" and popular opinion. In terms of the real bird, of course, they're out after prey; in terms of towns, they're out to achieve their goals, to ensure their vision becomes reality.

Eagle communities see opportunities that other communities are unable to see—or are afraid to take. Eagle communities know their own weaknesses and capitalize on their strengths. They have strategic plans, both short-term and long-term, in place. Their plans may not be greater than any other town's, but Eagle communities know when to strike. Focused on prosperity and growth, they become leaders and models in the process of achieving their maximum potential.

Of course, not every town falls neatly into one of these categories. In many cases there are internal struggles within towns; you might have a mixture of three or even all four types represented within local leaders, the business sector and private citizens. Many times a town seems stuck in neutral because it's

Attitude in Action

In real estate, the key might be location, location, location, but Douglas, Georgia, didn't let its less-than-ideal location hamper its growth. Located 51 miles from the nearest interstate, Douglas has not allowed this perceived disadvantage to stunt its impressive growth.

Like many small communities, Douglas had difficulties during the early 1980s. Then Wal-Mart located a distribution center hub in Douglas, citing its available labor and a strong work ethic as deciding factors. Douglas hasn't slowed down since. From 1996 to 2001, the town added 2,016 new manufacturing jobs and 12 new industries and saw many of its existing industries expand. One in four people is employed in manufacturing compared to the state average of only one in 11. The entire economy of Douglas has boomed as a result. Saralyn Stafford, president of the local chamber of commerce, said in late 2002, "The chamber last year had 64 ribbon-cuttings for new businesses. And we've been averaging two per week this year."

Here are examples of other towns that, like Douglas, radiate a can-do attitude.

- Newberry, South Carolina: Newberry pulled out all the stops for a site-selection project that located a Komatsu manufacturing plant in that town after more than 50 towns in 20 states were considered.
- Norfolk, Nebraska: Seeing the need for updated technology in order to survive, Norfolk built a $5 million state-of-the-art Lifelong Learning Center (with $1 million donated by hometown celebrity Johnny Carson).
- Marion, Illinois: Marion has aggressively courted more than 800 jobs for its citizens using a variety of methods, including Tax Increment Financing (TIF). In 2003 Marion planned to add a new TIF on 100 acres with proposed projects totaling $100 million in new investment, 200 new jobs and $50 million in new retail sales.
- Waverly, Ohio: www.cityofwaverly.net tells a lot about this friendly and progressive town. The mayor's page exemplifies this small town's can-do attitude with praise for his staff and an enthusiastic greeting of promise and action. Mayor Kelly, who earns $12,000 annually, has spread his enthusiasm throughout the town.
- Gillette, Wyoming: Started by homesteaders, ranchers and railroad hands, this remote town bills itself as the "Energy Capital of the Nation," and the local economic development group touts, "We've Got Energy. Come Join the Adventure!" In fact, local mines supply 30 percent of the need for coal in the United States. But the people of Gillette also recognize that their economic health depends upon continued growth and diversification of local industries. Local citizens banded together and purchased land to initiate Energy Park and Gillette Tech Center.

experiencing an internal tug-of-war between Mules and Moles on one side and maybe a few lone Eagles on the other (with a contingent of Jackals offering derisive commentary throughout the struggle). Successful towns keep internal struggles to a minimum and don't seriously impair their progress.

A Tale of Two Towns

Peru and LaSalle are quaint, old towns that grew up side-by-side along the Illinois River in northern Illinois. Over the years, they've grown together so much that you don't know where one ends and the other begins. Their names were so linked that, as a kid, I always thought the town was named LaSalle-Peru. LaSalle was always the big brother, dominating the retail and banking sectors of the two cities.

In the early 1960s, when Interstate 80 was built about three miles north of each city, there was much talk of what impact the interstate would have upon the local downtowns. Significant infrastructure would be required for either town to develop out by the interstate. Peru decided to go forward; LaSalle said no. A $100,000 commitment by the City of Peru officials was made to extend water and sewer service out to the new interstate.

Don Baker, mayor of Peru since 1965, remembers the controversy at the time. "*The Daily News-Tribune* and its editor thought that it was a crazy thing to do and stirred up a lot of negatives about us trying to develop all the way out to the interstate. Since the newspaper was LaSalle-based, it always seemed that they tended to side with LaSalle over Peru."

Barb Koch, executive director of the Illinois Valley Area Chamber of Commerce and Economic Development, recalls, "Most people thought that was too far from town; it was way out in the country. Mayor Baker and the Council did what they thought was right. "Since then, Mayor Baker has had minimal opposition because the community has seen how Peru has benefited from his visionary leadership. Baker's term ends in 2005, and he hopes to run for his eleventh term as mayor.

What happened to LaSalle? In 1970 LaSalle rang up about 10 percent more retail sales than Peru. Thirty years later, however, Peru's retail sales were almost six times that of its neighbor. That means Peru brings in almost $5 million per year in added local sales tax revenue that it can use for its citizens. In addition, many new industrial plants have located in Peru because of the interstate access. All this progress because of an investment of $100,000 made several decades ago.

Can-Do Characteristics

A can-do attitude is:

- **Visionary.** It sees possibilities that can't be seen otherwise.

- **Honest.** It does not "stick its head in the sand" when problems arise, but meets them head on.

- **Able to see beyond problems.** It acknowledges challenges and posits solutions.

- **Courageous.** It is not afraid of new ventures and is willing to take calculated risks.

- **Aware of strengths and its weaknesses.** It plans accordingly.

- **Capable of team-building.** It takes into account the good of all the people, not just a select few, and it draws on the strength of many to achieve goals.

- **Not egocentric.** It remains open to new suggestions for solutions and to consulting with others.

- **Intuitive.** It knows when the time is right to strike.

- **Focused.** It keeps its eye on the prize and adjusts its approach only as necessary to reach that prize.

- **Firm.** Although it carefully considers all criticism, it is not swayed by unfounded criticism or popular opinion provided by Mules, Moles and Jackals.

- **Relentless.** It does not give up.

Fostering a Can-Do Attitude

When its people are infused with a can-do attitude, a town that, for decades, has done nothing but limp along can gain new strength and develop wings like an eagle.

Hawarden, Iowa, provides one such example. In the mid 1990s, Hawarden (population: 2,478) ran into a brick wall during discussions with its local cable provider, headquartered in Denver. Aware of the increasing role that telecommunications would play in any future success, Hawarden wanted to up-grade its technology but was brushed off by the cable company.

Instead of shrugging and saying, "Gosh, that's too bad. I wish they would do something for us," the city took action. In 1994 the citizens of Hawarden over-whelmingly passed a referendum to create a municipal telecommunications/cable utility. With funding from a $4.5 million revenue bond, the city built its own hybrid fiber/coaxial network. This new technology helped to keep Coil Craft, a producer of parts for cellular phones with 250 employees, in town. And it has helped Hawarden move forward with positive momentum.

That's the ideal—when *all* the key players have a can-do attitude. In reality, most every town has its curmudgeons. A successful town doesn't let negative, short-sighted or fearful people stand in its way of progress. A *highly* successful town does even more: It wins over the curmudgeons, at least to the extent that even naysayers can play a part in helping the town prosper and move forward.

You don't have to be a great orator or a persuasive salesperson to con-vince others of the value of a can-do attitude. The most effective way to foster such an attitude is to simply live it, to make it an integral part of your life. Of course, having an Eagle attitude—and helping your community adopt that at-titude—is easier said than done. You can begin winning over people by using the PEOPLE approach:

- **Plan**—Make a specific plan to win over those who will, or already do, oppose the project.
- **Enlist allies**—Include those in your community who share your en-thusiasm for the project and see its potential for the town, as well as the key players from outside the community.
- **Observe opponents**—Know and respect the objections of those who oppose the project, and be ready to counter objections with solid reasons why the project is worth pursuing.
- **Present the plan**—Paint a clear picture of how the town will pros-per by taking on the project.
- **Lead by example**—Be visionary, acknowledge problems, propose solutions, take calculated risks, build teams, be open to sugges-tions, stay focused and never give up.
- **Engage others**—Involve many people in the project as early as possible. An effective way to win over an opponent is to give him or her a role to play in the project's success, and allow that per-son to have ownership in it.

More specifically, here's how this six-stage approach works:

Plan. Before you can win people over, you must have a specific plan to win them to. You can't expect people to come over to your side, or to adopt your way of thinking, if you can't show them how they will benefit.

For example, maybe you see an opportunity to recruit a software development company and perhaps even build a high-tech center that will house several technology firms. But your town has not been a "high-tech" town; you need to convince people of the sagacity of this new direction by preparing reports and figures that forecast the financial future for your town if it makes such a move.

Enlist Allies. Drum up support from two groups: those in your community of a like mind and those involved in the venture outside your community (for example, executives of a business you are trying to recruit). In this stage you are gathering strength and momentum for your plan. When other key people endorse your plan, its credibility rises and its potential gains dimension.

In keeping with the example above, your allies in bringing high-tech companies to your town might include a forward-thinking banker, a chamber member who previously lived in another high-tech town and executives of one or more of the companies you are interested in attracting. Each ally can bring his or her perspective to the venture; the plan becomes more than one person's desire, and the benefits can be seen from varying vantage points. Your plan begins to take shape and draws energy from your allies.

Observe Opponents. Your "opponents" in this case might be the mayor, the town council or anyone else opposed to the idea that you intend to proffer. Your intent, of course, is to win over your opponents, making them not only your allies but also equal partners in bringing about the desired change in your town. To do this, you need to observe your opponents, identify what might fuel their reluctance to accept your plan, and understand what might influence their negative attitude. This is not an exercise in justifying your own opinion, but in understanding and respecting the opinions of others.

For example, the opponents you want to turn into teammates may have various reasons why bringing in high-tech business is not good or feasible for your town: The financial outlay is too big; the economy is too unstable; the companies you're interested in recruiting are too young; the workforce for such companies is not in place in town; the town has not ventured into the high-tech world before; high-tech companies might clash with, or threaten the dominance of, already entrenched industries; and so on. By understanding and then addressing their apprehensions, concerns and motives—not brow-beating them into submission—you can rally opponents to your side.

Present the Plan. Understanding others' qualms (and the thinking behind them) aids you in preparing to present your plan most effectively. At this stage, you first attempt to win over your opponents. You have lined up your allies, you're armed with financial analyses and strategies that show the specifics of how your plan will benefit your town, and you have considered the best ways to break down the resistance you face.

Here's an important distinction between a can-do attitude and Pollyanna-ism. The latter is born of blind optimism, the kind that is endearing but often groundless. Sometimes, such optimism is well-served; at other times it is ill-advised. As a result, you can't fully trust a person with a Pollyanna outlook because *everything* looks rosy to such a person, and *everything* will always work out in this person's eyes.

A person with a can-do attitude, on the other hand, balances his or her optimism with a heavy dose of reality. In fact, the optimism of can-do people *stems from* the reality of opportunities that they envision and research. Can-do people don't blindly go down any path, eagerly inviting others to join them in the journey. They assay the situation, envision how to enhance and grow their town, and then share that vision—aided by hard facts—with others who can't help but catch the can-do fever.

Presenting a plan is much like making a sales pitch. The pitch, however, must be grounded in fact, clearly present the opportunities, address the concerns and risks, specify how problems can be avoided or solved, and explain why the risks are worth taking.

In presenting a plan to build a high-tech center in your town, you wouldn't fill the meeting room with warm platitudes, good cheer and engaging optimism; you'd confidently present hard facts, real people and companies and the specific benefits of bringing those corporations to town. You would paint a clear picture of how the town would prosper by making the moves you are suggesting, address the risks involved and the concerns people might have and focus on how the plan would benefit the town.

Lead by Example. When people see the can-do attitude in action, they are more likely to change their minds—especially if you experience minor victories along the way and thus provide positive outcomes for others to reflect upon. Leading by example encompasses being visionary, acknowledging problems, posing solutions, raising possibilities, taking calculated risks, building a team, being open to new suggestions, keeping your eyes on the prize, being undeterred by popular opinion and never giving up.

For instance, winning over civic leaders to build a high-tech center would be aided by your acknowledgement and assessment of the objections to such a plan, followed by the details of a low-interest loan the local bank is willing to offer, a summary of clerical and administrative positions the new company can offer to town residents, and the promise of the company president to offer low-cost computer training to local residents. You could report such findings only after working behind the scenes, meeting with key people (the banker and the company president), mulling over known or suspected concerns that will be raised and coming up with solutions. If you don't do this type of homework, naysayers will find it easier to shoot down your proposal to bring a new type of industry to town.

Engage Others. The final step in fostering a can-do attitude is to actively involve others as early as possible in your endeavors. Beyond enlisting allies, you need to get key people on board, even if those people are likely to oppose your proposal at first. This keeps in mind the team-building process that is so vital to small towns: After all, you're in it for the town's benefit, not your own.

For example, as you talk to the banker about the loan for the high-tech center and talk with the software company president about jobs, revenue and computer training for the community, bring along several key players from town who need to be won over but aren't firmly opposed to the notion. Let them experience first-hand the possibilities and solutions to potential problems that come with the project's territory. There is strength in numbers; your report will be amplified by the approval of those whom you've managed to ·engage early in the process.

Who to engage and when is a gut call that you'll have to make. All is not lost, of course, if you try to engage someone early on and that person continues to be reluctant or negative, but you'll waste a lot of time and energy if you have to continually convince the same people to support your efforts. Once a project has been formally approved, engage many people in realizing the project to its completion.

Winning initial approval is one issue; garnering and maintaining ongoing support and enthusiasm is another. To accomplish the latter, call on people to keep the project progressing and on track to achieve its potential. In this way, those who may have opposed the idea earlier now have ownership in it—and they've experienced a can-do attitude firsthand.

Tombstone, Arizona: Too Tough to Die

Tombstone, Arizona, is literally in the middle of nowhere. All of its natural resources—silver and gold—were mined out years ago. The town has even burned to the ground twice. Fortunately, Mayor Dusty Escapule and his fellow citizens didn't know they were supposed to close down and blow away like most of the old Wild West mining towns.

In fact, the town's motto says a great deal about the residents' can-do spirit: "The Town Too Tough to Die." Tombstone plays upon its colorful history of a Wild West town with daily gunfights in its authentic downtown historical district. It attracts more than 500,000 visitors per year, some from as far away as Europe and Asia.

In addition to serving as mayor, Escapule operates the horse-drawn stage-coaches and covered wagons for guided tours of his hometown. He says his biggest challenge has been upgrading the infrastructure to accommodate all of Tombstone's visitors. When he became mayor, the town only had 150,000 gallons of water capacity; it now has more than 1.6 million gallons.

Key #2: Shape Your Vision

V ision marks the roadmap to success; it takes into account the destination, the surrounding terrain, and the roadblocks and hazards along the way. With vision, you can determine the best way to reach your destination.

Vision is as important to a town's success as it is to an individual's or to a corporation's. In fact, vision often makes the difference between a ghost town and a booming town.

One Person's Dream

The poet Carl Sandburg once said, "Nothing happens unless first a dream." And Walt Disney believed, "If you can dream it, you can do it." Both of these famous Americans were not only able to articulate a vision but also able to make their visions happen. The vision for a town starts with one person, such as J. Irwin Miller of Columbus, Indiana.

You'll find Columbus in the center of a triangle formed by Indianapolis, Louisville and Cincinnati. With an economy based on farming and milling, it slowly grew in the last half of the 19th century and was not really distinguishable from any other small Midwestern town. Then, in 1942, the First Christian Church dedicated its new building designed by Finnish architect Eliel Saarinen. This structure, which signaled the beginning of modern architecture in Columbus, was followed in the 1950s by construction of a new bank, also designed by Saarinen, and a school.

In 1957, J. Irwin Miller, chairman of the board of the Cummins Engine Company, now Cummins Inc., headquartered in Columbus, offered to pay the architect's fee for any new school designed by an architect from a list compiled by the Cummins Engine Foundation, now The Cummins Foundation. This vision for high-quality architecture expanded to include public buildings and churches. Columbus now has more than 65 buildings—including a hospital, city hall, post office, jail, public housing, library and even a fire station—designed by world-renowned architects.

Spurred by the vision of a few, Columbus changed its look so radically, and with such style, that the American Institute of Architects has listed it sixth in the nation for architectural innovation and design—behind Chicago, New York, San Francisco, Boston and Washington, D.C. Not bad company for a city of 39,000. And all it took to get started was one person's vision.

Columbus is vibrant and growing—and understands that a community must constantly reinvent itself. During the "Rust Belt Recession" of the 1980s, Columbus saw that being largely dependent upon one company was not prudent in the long term. It formed a public-private economic development board to trumpet the town's advantages to other firms. Since 1985, more than 40 new companies have started operations in the town, creating more than 10,000 new jobs. Several companies from Europe and Asia have chosen Columbus as their beachhead plant into the U.S. market, giving this small town an international feel not often found in towns of the same size.

Creating a Vision

The architectural splendor of Columbus, Indiana, resulted from the collective vision that its civic and business leaders and residents had for the town. Their success didn't just happen. It was crafted. It was planned. It was inspired by people who dared to dream big.

Shifting Gears: From Passion to Profit

Mike Yager was infatuated with Corvettes as a teenager, but he didn't simply fantasize about turning his passion into a profitable business. In 1974, at the age of 24, he borrowed $500 from a local bank in Effingham, Illinois, and started selling Corvette patches, jackets, shirts, glasses and owner's manuals at auto events and through a one-page catalog sheet. His company, Mid America Designs, now employs 140, mails six million catalogs annually and does $50 million in sales per year.

Mike's vision for his company and hometown is "to become the Branson of the Collector Car Market in the U.S." The company has expanded into Porsche and Volkswagen, has its own museum and holds three weekend car festivals each year. The festivals attract more than 10,000 collector automobiles and 50,000 people to Effingham. Yager, who dreams of adding additional venues and businesses to his auto-collecting megaplex, is proudest of "having created tremendous opportunities for so many people in my hometown."

Oxford, Mississippi: A Literary Tradition Continues

Having the University of Mississippi and William Faulkner, a Nobel Prize Winner for Literature, as nurturing influences has allowed the small town of Oxford, Mississippi, to evolve into the literary center of the South. Many writers now make their home in Oxford, where the annual Faulkner and Yoknapatawpha Conference is held at the University of Mississippi each August. Participants from around the world attend the conference and visit Rowan Oak, Faulkner's home.

In 1979 Richard Howorth returned to Oxford from Washington, D.C., to open a bookstore that would help elevate the image of Oxford as a place of culture, literacy and broad-mindedness. As Howorth says, "Oxford had been wrongly viewed so many times, at so many different historic junctures; maybe this will help compensate."

Starting with $10,000 in savings and another $10,000 borrowed from a local bank, Howorth opened Square Books on the second floor of a downtown building. With adept promotion and word-of-mouth advertising, Square Books eventually became a cultural focal point in the community. In the early 1990s, working with the Center for the Study of Southern Culture at Ole Miss, Square Books started the Oxford Conference for the Book. This three-day gathering of writers, poets, editors and publishers brings in thousands of enthusiasts each year and has helped to cement Oxford's literary reputation.

In some cases, dreams may appear as foolishness to those in neighboring towns. Imagine the reaction of folks of Cashmere, Washington, when they heard that neighboring Leavenworth, undergoing an economic crisis, decided to turn itself into the replica of a Bavarian village. "An economic crisis? Try an identity crisis!" some probably scoffed. And who in the music industry would have picked tiny Branson, Missouri, as the logical choice for the live musical capital of the world? No one—except the folks from Branson. To them it seemed a reasonable thing to do. So they made it happen.

Leavenworth's vision was born of necessity; the town needed to do something, and do it quickly. Fortunately, the town crafted its vision wisely. In contrast, Branson wasn't forced to "do something." It *chose* to do something. Branson's success grew from a vision that seemed outlandish to many, but very doable to those involved.

Genius, Einstein said, is one percent inspiration and 99 percent perspiration. That one percent—in which the vision resides—makes all the difference. It guides the other 99 percent, giving life and meaning to the effort. Without the inspiration, without the vision, the perspiration amounts to nothing more than sweat.

Vision alone won't make you successful, however. Visions for towns have fallen painfully short at times. Take the rather odd case of Braselton, Georgia. The town was part of the land that actress Kim Basinger purchased in 1990 with the help of a $20 million pension fund from Ameritech. The land she purchased bordered Gwynnett County which, in the late 1980s, was the fastest growing county in the United States. Basinger, who was born in nearby Athens, Georgia, reportedly wanted to transform Braselton into a creative arts center.

The investment went sour in 1993 when Basinger filed for bankruptcy after a judge ordered her to pay Main Line Pictures $8.1 million for backing out of a verbal commitment to star in a movie. Although she appealed the ruling and eventually reached an out-of-court settlement with Main Line, Basinger was forced to sell her interest in Braselton for $1 million. Part of the problem resided in apparently poor planning by Basinger, her brother (who was the town's chief operating officer) and the management team of the Ameritech pension fund. The new management team, which came on board after the 1990 purchase, decided the town didn't fit well with its plans, balked at providing additional capital to finance development projects and wished to distance itself from Basinger's court problems. Braselton found itself caught between a celebrity and a large financial management team. The best-laid plans that fueled the purchase were judged, just a few years later, to be lacking in vision, and the plug was pulled.

Similarly, in the 19th century many towns sprang up around natural springs, which were rich in minerals and viewed as having healing powers. Sailor Springs, Illinois, was so successful it boasted of having the first concrete road and telephone system in the state. French Lick, Indiana, drew visitors from all over the United States. Hot Springs, Arkansas, counted many U.S. presidents among its frequent guests. Today, Sailor Springs has fewer than 100 residents, and French Lick is struggling to reinvent itself. Only Hot Springs developed a total package to continue as a thriving community.

Thomasville, Georgia: Meshing Past and Future

Thomasville, Georgia, an old "Southern Plantation Town," became internationally known during the late 1880s as the "Original Winter Resort of the South" because of its luxuriously appointed hotels. Northerners by the thousands came to breathe the town's healthy, pine-scented air. Many of the hotels and mansions built during the Gilded Age remain as museums, shops and homes. Tourism spawns many jobs; however, high-tech industries generally offer better-paying jobs.

Thomasville recognized that it needed a more advanced telecommunications infrastructure to build upon its success, so it bought the utilities that serviced the town and upgraded them to world-class standards. As a result, several companies have moved operations and plants to the community, including Flower Industries (a food-processing company) and the earth-moving giant Caterpillar. Ross Ware, Caterpillar's local manager, says "Thomasville has many features that you don't expect in a town this size, with a technological infrastructure and a mind-set to see the future being two of them."

Building on Strengths

Different towns have different strengths. Some strengths come from the surrounding natural resources—such as natural springs—and some from the people and industries within the town. A partial listing of strengths that towns have built upon includes: climate, land, lakes and forests, parks and recreational areas, proximity to big cities, local businesses and industries, and unique qualities and features.

Florida's Wakulla Springs State Park, located in the state's panhandle, features one of the world's largest and deepest freshwater springs. On a clear water day, the park's glass-bottom boat allows visitors to see fish and fossilized mastodon bones in the depths of the springs. The pristine river and sanctuary provides a natural habitat for alligators, birds, turtles, deer and turkeys and attracts thousands of migrating waterfowl during the winter months.

Two of the more unusual events that take place in Wakulla County are the Blue Crab Festival during the first weekend of May, when the area's famous hard-shell blue crabs draw in 20,000 people, and the Monarch Butterfly

Festival in the fall of the year. Thousands of people come to view the butterflies as they prepare to migrate across the Gulf of Mexico to their wintering grounds in the mountains of Mexico. Wakulla County and the towns within it, including Sopchoppy, Panacea and St. Marks, play off their natural resources.

Hendersonville, North Carolina, nestled in the scenic Dupont State Forest, is a town whose leaders decided about 50 years ago that they needed to do something to differentiate their town from every other small town in the state. They drew on their native strength of being the seventh-largest producer of apples in the United States and began the Hendersonville Apple Festival; the four-day event brings in more than 250,000 people each year. The success of the Apple Festival inspired the town to create other events, such as the Garden Jubilee over Memorial Day weekend; "Music on Main" every Friday evening during the summer; family-oriented summer dances every Monday; and annual art shows, antique shows and Sidewalk Chalk Art Shows.

For Decatur, Texas, proximity to Dallas and Fort Worth became a selling point. Located only 30 miles from the metropolitan area, the town promotes that nearness as well as its lower costs and positive business climate in trying to attract new companies and residents. Decatur is one of the few towns whose city and chamber Web sites (www.decaturtx.com and www.decaturtx.org) have a unified look and very similar web addresses, something more towns could benefit from. Another community that capitalizes on its proximity to a metropolitan area is Sanford, Maine. Sanford, which sits between the Portsmouth-Rochester, New Hampshire MSA and the Portland, Maine MSA, boasts a small-town character and relatively low housing costs compared to the nearby metro areas.

Hidden Strengths

If you're a small town in southern Florida, your strengths—at least the natural ones—are sunshine and warm weather. If you're a small town in the Rocky Mountains in Colorado, your natural strengths are mountains and snow. If you're a town in the Land of 10,000 Lakes, some of your strengths are water sports and fishing. But what if you're a town in the middle of Kansas, with no striking natural resources surrounding you? What if your strengths don't just leap out and display themselves for the world to see? What if you can't find a single strength upon which to build?

Don't panic. Remember, *some* strengths come from a town's natural resources and surroundings. Other strengths come from a town's *people* and its industries (either current or potential ones). A community's vision can be built around its natural resources, but it can also be built around the ingenuity and passion of its people who, given nothing with which to work, literally shape their vision out of nothing.

Think of an artist working with a blank canvas. That canvas holds exciting possibilities, because it can become anything. So, too, within reason, can a town.

Fort Payne, Alabama, offers one example. When its coal and iron industries declined in the early 1900s, three local businessmen started the W.B. Davis Hosiery Mill with 30 knitting machines and 12 finishing machines. Back in 1907, their goal was to expand to 300 machines and 800 employees.

Today Fort Payne is known as the "Sock Capital of the World" because 6,000 employees working in hosiery factories in the town and surrounding DeKalb County produce about 12 million pairs of socks each *week*. Five of Fort Payne's top 10 companies are involved in the hosiery business, and many ancillary businesses have sprung up. What's more, most of the sock-making equipment used throughout the world originated in Fort Payne.

Wall, South Dakota: Simply Phenomenal

Were it not for the vision of Dorothy Hustead, most people would never have heard of tiny Wall, South Dakota, located near the Badlands National Park, the Black Hills and Mount Rushmore. She and her pharmacist husband purchased the Wall Drug Store in 1931—not the best time to begin a business. The Great Depression was just beginning, and most of Wall's farmers (the bedrock of the community) were on the verge of bankruptcy. Business went from bad to worse.

One hot July afternoon in 1936, as she watched a steady stream of cars drive past, Dorothy had a revelation that significantly affected her life. The people in those cars, she figured, *had* to be thirsty. One thing she and her husband had to offer was water. Why not put up some signs offering those tired and thirsty travelers some free ice water?

Before the Husteads had finished erecting a series of signs outside of town, thirsty travelers were already stopping at their drugstore for the free water. They put up more signs, Wall's fame grew, and now—thanks to word-of-mouth advertising and clever bumper stickers and highway billboards—more than 20,000 visitors a day stop by Wall Drug Store.

Learning from Others

Consider the publishing industry. Each publishing house has its own strengths and attributes, but all successful publishing houses operate in similar fashion. Their uniqueness is found in their products. Or look at the auto industry. Different automakers produce similar, yet distinct, cars. All offer certain necessary features—four wheels, an engine and a steering wheel—but they don't produce the exact same cars.

And so it is with towns. Certain approaches and visions have helped some communities prosper, and other towns can learn much from their neighbors as they begin to fashion their own approach and vision. No individual, company or town has a copyright on success, so learn from the success other towns enjoy and apply the lessons to your own community. Typically, people in small towns love to talk about themselves and their success. They aren't afraid to admit when they use something from another town, and they are more than willing to help other towns achieve success as well.

Effingham, Illinois' mayor, Bob Utz, viewed a sculpture program in Cedar Rapids, Iowa, and brought the idea back home. Effingham's sculpture program attracts sculptors from all over the Midwest, who work in media ranging from stainless steel to wood to stained glass. Now, dozens of sculptures grace Effingham's quaint downtown.

One endeavor worthy of emulation involves Ruby Ranch, Colorado, which developed its own high-speed broadband network when Qwest did not fulfill townspeople's desire to enter the Internet age. Carl Oppedahl had moved to Ruby Ranch in 1997 and began requesting high-speed phone service. When his requests were repeatedly countered with excuses about the high cost of providing anything but a slow dial-up service to the small town, Oppedahl and a dozen of his neighbors set up the Ruby Ranch Internet Cooperative Association. Despite the many obstacles placed in its path, the association persevered and set up its own broadband network in 2001.

Realizing Your Vision

Once your community vision is in place, you need to develop a plan to bring it to fruition. This plan is split into four phases: setting goals, working toward those goals, evaluating your progress and making adjustments as necessary. Take a look at each phase as it applies to your town's vision.

1. Set Goals. Goals are tools to help you get to where you want to be and accomplish what you wish to achieve. You might have a grand vision, but without goals to guide you along the way and to act as checkpoints, your road to achieving that vision might be a lot longer or you might veer off course. Set realistic goals that will help you achieve your vision and are challenging but also, with focus and effort, reachable. Here are a few examples:

- **Morehead City, North Carolina**, located in the southernmost part of the Outer Banks, was historically dependent upon the military. In 1971 a group of community and business leaders met to discuss how to have planned, orderly growth in the area. They established the Carteret County Economic Development Council with the goal of recruiting and retaining industry and promoting high-wage, year-round employment. Several years later, Don Kirkman, president of the Carteret County Economic Development Council from 1990 to 2000, saw a niche market that Morehead City could fill. He developed a vision and leveraged the city's unique location to turn it into one of the leading marine science centers in the world. Duke University, North Carolina State, the University of North Carolina, the National Marine Fisheries Service, the National Weather Service, and the North Carolina Division of Marine Fisheries all maintain laboratories in the county. Morehead City also capitalized on its unique location to create several industrial and high-tech parks to enhance employment opportunities for its residents. Although the military still accounts for 14 percent of its population, Morehead City has successfully diversified its economic base.

- To boost local retail sales in **Ponchatoula, Louisiana**, the chamber of commerce organized the Ponchatoula Professional and Business Expo, giving local companies a chance to exhibit their products and services. Launched in 1998, the annual event has grown from fewer than 100 visitors in that first year to more than 600 annually. Businesses report they have received recognition—and increased sales—by exhibiting at the event.

Make your goals specific and measurable. A vague—and useless—goal is saying, "I want our town to prosper this year." What resident doesn't want this? And, more to the point, how would this goal help residents take the steps to improve their town? It wouldn't. Here's a better attempt: "I want our community to have better employment figures and income than it did last year."

At least this provides a bit of a measuring stick and a direction, but the goal remains vague and ineffectual. A measurable and effective goal would be, "I want our community to drop one point in its unemployment rate and increase per-capita income by $2,000 this year." This gives your economic development team and civic leaders something specific to shoot for.

Another example of a vague vs. a measurable goal is this:

Vague: "We want our town to attract more downtown shoppers."

Measurable: "We want to refurbish the downtown shopping area by landscaping the town square, putting in new sidewalks on Main Street, fixing up the storefronts, placing comfortable benches along the street, and creating three mini-parks adjacent to downtown to attract more shoppers. As a result of these changes, we want to attract more shoppers to the downtown area, increasing sales by five percent per year."

Measurable, specific goals hold you accountable. They let you know where you stand and keep you going until you've achieved what you set out to. Vague goals don't stick with you, because you never know if you've really achieved them or not; they're too subjective and open to interpretation to be meaningful.

Finally, ensure your goals are performance-oriented. Such goals are more meaningful than outcome-oriented goals; you have control over your own performance, but not necessarily over the *outcome* of your performance. For example, even if your community *can* realistically become a big festival town, your goal should be performance-oriented ("We want to create three annual festivals within the next three years") rather than outcome-oriented ("We want to supplant Hendersonville as one of the biggest tourist attractions in southwest North Carolina"). You can control how you develop your town's vision; you can't control what other towns achieve.

Performance-oriented goals help your town focus on its own strengths and resources and on its own achievements. Such goals help you ignore external distractions—the things you can't control. That's not to say you're not *aware* of your surroundings and what affects your town: It just says that your community focuses on what it can control and sets its sights on improving itself.

2. Work Toward Goals. Once you have a goal in place, consider the specific steps that you must take to reach the goal. Make the steps measurable, realistic and performance-oriented. Some goals take weeks or months to accomplish; others take years. To achieve your goal, you need to reach certain steps along the way. These steps act as checkpoints. They are really mini-goals; reaching each one assures you that you're on the right path and on schedule.

Saving Main Street

Main Street used to be the focal point of the downtown area, where you'd find retailers and service businesses, restaurants and cafes, clubs and theaters and prime apartments on the floors above the shops. Anyone who wanted to be part of what was happening in town would head to Main Street—especially on Saturday nights, when Main Street provided the backdrop for a thriving social center. Every road, it seemed, headed downtown and ran into Main Street.

Those same roads now lead to highways and interstates that take people to distant malls and shopping centers. The shops and stores on Main Street have grown old and feeble, a remnant of the past; many of the Main Street establishments have not been able to withstand the transformation brought about by improved highway systems.

"Going Out of Business Sale" and "Closed—For Good" signs spread across the nation's Main Streets like a fatal disease. In town after town, downtown retail businesses closed, shoppers dwindled and property values plunged. Apathy followed. Neglected buildings, boarded-up storefronts and trash-strewn streets reinforced in people's minds that the downtown area was irrelevant and had no hope of ever returning to its past glory.

Several towns, however, have decided not to let their downtowns disappear without a fight. Many towns have succeeded in saving their often historical buildings along Main Street and transformed their downtown areas into shopping venues that can't be found at the large chain operations. Some towns have revived their commercial core and provided a sense of place and community life, through farmer's markets, art centers, outdoor performances and other activities. Towns that have done particularly well at reviving their downtowns include: Grass Valley, California; Hollister, California; Thomasville, Georgia; Statesville, North Carolina; Wooster, Ohio; Durant, Oklahoma; Stillwater, Oklahoma; Corsicana, Texas; Kerrville, Texas; Mt. Pleasant, Texas; Rocky Mount, Virginia; Menomonie, Wisconsin; and Morgantown, West Virginia.

Most community goals are team-oriented; they involve the efforts of many people along the way. In this case you need to get everyone on board (if you are in charge); everyone needs to feel ownership of the goal and understand the part they have to play to reach the goal. Such cases call for a coordinated effort, but the process is still the same: You set your goal, determine the specific steps to take and begin taking one step at a time.

Break down a goal into chunks that you can use as a focus for each week. That is, if you have a project that's scheduled to be completed in six months, what do you need to accomplish by the second month? By the fourth month? From there, break it down further. To be on target by the end of the second month, what do you need to do in week 1? Week 2? This not only gives you a focus for that week, it lets you know if you're on schedule. The more you divide your goal into measurable, realistic and performance-oriented steps, the more tuned in you are to the project and the less likely you are to get off schedule.

Picayune, Mississippi, provides an example of a town that knows how to effectively work toward a goal. The Picayune Downtowners Association was organized in 1996 to promote business in Picayune and to preserve the integrity of downtown businesses. The association turned the Picayune Street Fair, which began as a six-business event in 1966, into a bi-annual event, which now draws more than 250 vendors from the local area and from eight to 10 nearby states. More than 30,000 visitors attend each fair, and the Picayune Street Fair is recognized by Southern Tourism as a Top 20 Event in the Southeast.

3. Evaluate Your Progress. When you break your goal down into specific, measurable, small steps, you can easily monitor your progress. At the end of each time period, note what tasks you have accomplished and what remains to be done.

Some goals have natural checkpoints along the way that are a month or so apart from one another. That's why it's helpful to break the work that leads up to each natural checkpoint into week-long units with specific goals; otherwise, three or four weeks can slip by without much progress—and without much concern about the lack of progress. At that point it might be difficult to make up the lost ground. The smaller and more measurable the steps, the easier it is to evaluate your progress and stay on schedule.

4. Make Adjustments. Adjust your schedule or your steps if you find you are off target. If the project or goal isn't time-sensitive—if a delay is not a critical issue—then perhaps you can continue on, with no adjustments, even if you find yourself off schedule. If it is time-sensitive, adjust your schedule to make up for lost time.

You might find that you set too fast a pace for yourself in your timeline—and can't accomplish the steps as quickly. Perhaps the delay stems from things that are out of your control or because other people are necessarily involved. Whatever the reason, you'll need to make adjustments if the goal is time-sensitive. Again, if the goal you set is realistic in its statement and in its timeline, then you shouldn't be too far off. Goals most often go awry when they are unrealistic in content or in their allotted timeframe.

Realize, too, that little of life goes exactly as planned. Be prepared to make minor adjustments along the way toward reaching your goal. Minor adjustments are common and necessary. It's when you are forced to make major adjustments that you should reassess your goal and consider whether it's realistic and practical.

Key #3: Leverage Your Resources

W hen you build on your town's strengths and resources, you make prosperity and growth real possibilities.

Consider Jackson, Wyoming (often called "Jackson Hole"), a former fur trading village nestled at the edge of the towering Grand Teton Mountains. Now a stylish retreat for celebrities, the town of 8,500 has reinvented itself repeatedly to take full advantage of its resources.

In the mid-1800s David E. Jackson and other trappers began gathering in the small settlement to trade their wares. By 1900 the town, which had become known as Jackson's Hole, concentrated on cattle ranching and had a population of 64. When ranching proved less than profitable, Jackson became home to "dude ranches." Dozens of these ranches spouted up between 1908 and the early 1930s. Many wealthy and influential "dudes" began to view Jackson as a tourist destination because of its natural beauty. In 1926, John D. Rockefeller, in a controversial move, began buying ranches between Jackson and Yellowstone; this land would eventually become the nucleus for the Grand Teton National Park. Yet while tourists flocked to Jackson in the summer, the town went into hibernation each fall.

In 1940 the first rope tow was opened on Snow King, followed by the first lift in 1946. When the second ski area, Teton Village, opened in 1965, Jackson was on its way to becoming a year-round tourist destination. Today, more than three million people per year visit Jackson Hole for its natural beauty and cultural events. (If you're there the first weekend of June, be sure to attend the annual Paw-to-Paw Competition to crown the best Frisbee-catching dog in Jackson.)

Although its scenery is not as spectacular as Jackson's, Holmes County, Ohio, has been just as successful in using its natural resources to its benefit. Situated in the north-central part of the state, Holmes County has fertile soil, natural rolling hills and Millersburg (population: 3,326)—the largest Amish settlement in the country. It also has the distinction of having a crime rate of zero.

More than half of the county's 38,000 residents trace their heritage to the Amish, who have expanded beyond farming into many cottage industries. The available workforce attracted other industries, and today many national companies manufacture everything from pill bottles to electronic control systems in the community. Yet, even as the new industries flourish, Amish cheese, still delivered in traditional milk cans from the local farms, and furniture making continue to play an important role in the county's overall economy.

Much to Work With

Jackson and Holmes County are leveraging their main resources: the natural beauty of the Tetons and the fertile soil of Ohio. Other strengths and resources might include the following categories:

Current industries, businesses and institutions. These usually represent the "bread and butter" of your community because they provide the majority of jobs and income. These employment bases may be concentrated in one field. Many a town, for example, becomes known primarily as a manufacturing center, or a high-tech area, or a college town. This is neither good nor bad. What's important is that the employment base contains enough employers so that, if one or two pull out, the community isn't left high and dry.

Most towns have a mix of employers—manufacturers, retailers, schools, medical facilities and so on. This is suitable to a healthy employment climate and is often more attractive to outsiders who might be considering moving to your town, because they see a wider range of goods and services and a healthy employment base.

That said, a town with employers in multiple fields often has a particular strength (a major employer) in one of those fields. A town can leverage its past success by attracting more companies within that same field. As your economic development team considers a plan for growth, one of the first items on the agenda ought to be assessing and building on current strengths. Manufacturers are more likely to be interested in your town if they see that other manufacturers are successful in it.

At times, certain industries that have traditionally done well in your town may be drying up because of something happening within that industry (or within that company). If the industry itself is beginning to wane, look at building up other industries within your town. For example, if you've traditionally been a manufacturing town, with the majority of the employment in the declining steel industry, look to diversify into something related, such as plastics, or to build up your service industries (health services, social services and so on),

Manufacturing Jobs = Small Town Prosperity = Lower Taxes

Manufacturers are the backbone of many small towns. Manufacturing jobs have traditionally paid well and supported other businesses in the community. A study done by the Illinois Chamber of Commerce (What 100 New Jobs Mean to a Community, 1993) shows that 100 new manufacturing jobs in a community lead to:

- 415 more jobs
- $12,700,000 more personal income per year
- $5,000,000 more bank deposits
- Seven additional retail establishments
- $7,700,000 more retail sales
- $540,000 increased tax revenue
- $2,000,000 more service receipts

In the 397 agurbs identified in this book, the number of manufacturing jobs grew by 25,455 (2 percent) during the 1990s, while the United States lost 2,176,073 (–10.6 percent) manufacturing jobs. And these manufacturing jobs paid 71.7 percent more than retail jobs ($618.87 per week compared to $360.53 per week).

In their book *Manufacturing Works: The Vital Link Between Production and Prosperity,* (Dearborn Financial Publishing, Inc., 2002) Fred Zimmerman and Dave Beal look at 690 U.S. counties with more than 4,800 manufacturing employees in 1995. They found that local and county taxes declined dramatically with an increase in manufacturing. Those with 10 percent of their jobs in manufacturing averaged $1,000 per capita in taxes; those with 30 percent averaged $650; and those with 40 percent averaged $562.

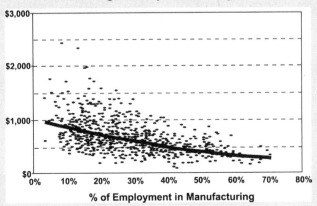

Manufacturing Intensity and Per-Capita Taxes

% of Employment in Manufacturing

your construction industry or your retail trade industry—whatever industries are prospering and are forecast to do well in the future. Or, develop a narrower niche within a larger commodity or type of product.

Here are two other examples:

- **Apalachicola, Florida,** has Apalachicola Bay, one of the cleanest and most productive waters in the nation. More than 90 percent of Florida's oysters are harvested there, producing more than $14 million for the local economy, providing over 1,000 jobs and offering more than 1.4 million pounds of oyster meat, all shucked in local seafood houses.

- **Corning, New York,** is a manufacturing town that made a name for itself in glass production. The company and town evolved from flat glass to glass cookware and then moved into fiber optics, which became a new growth industry. Many smaller companies have since sprung up in Corning, developing out of glassmaking's technological talent pool.

To leverage your current businesses, industries and institutions, you need to understand what has worked in the past, have a sense for what will be successful in the future and have an ability to work with current and potential employers to expand your employment base and strengthen your town. You want to keep that "bread and butter" coming—but sometimes you have to switch to a new brand of bread. At other times, you simply want to increase the production of the same bread that has been feeding your community for decades.

Natural resources, such as lakes, beaches, mountains, and forests.

Hilton Head Island is a barrier reef, the second largest such Atlantic island after Long Island, New York, off the coast of South Carolina. The island, which is seven miles wide and 14 miles long, has been inhabited by Native American tribes, Southern plantation owners, escaped slaves and eventually an isolated group of "native" islanders who had their own language known as "Gullah."

In the 1950s, Charles Fraser, a young Yale-trained lawyer, talked his father into selling him the southern third of the island. In 1956 he persuaded the state to build a two-lane bridge to his new Sea Pines Plantation project. But Fraser's Sea Pines was unlike any other beach community, most of which featured small cottages perched atop cinder blocks. Fraser laid out a completely new community with the homes built away from the oceanfront and designed to blend into the natural pine forests. Golf courses, bike paths and hundreds of acres of nature preserves were part of the aesthetics. He said in an interview in *Southern Living* magazine, "I felt you could be economically successful developing this beach either way, ugly or beautiful. There's no law of economics that says ugliness pays. I selected beauty and set out to make it work economically."

Today, Hilton Head has 36,800 residents and hosts more than 2.5 million visitors each year. Fraser developed similar projects including Amelia Island Plantation in Florida, Kiawah Island Resort in South Carolina and the Palmas del Mar Resort in Puerto Rico. Other small towns that have profited from their natural beauty include:

- **Grants Pass, Oregon**, situated on the Rogue River and nestled between Crater Lake and the Cascade Mountain Range, and the Siskiyou National Forest and the Klamath Mountains.
- **Sandpoint, Idaho**, located near Lake Pend Oreille and in the Coeur d'Alene National Forest.
- **Newport, Tennessee**, with Douglas Lake on one side and the Appalachian Mountains and the Cherokee National Forest on the other.
- **Prescott, Arizona**, with the Prescott National Forest as its backdrop.
- **Clarkston, Washington**, featuring the rugged beauty of Hells Canyon, North America's deepest gorge.
- **Dawsonville, Georgia**, situated at the southern end of the Appalachian Trail and featuring a 729-foot waterfall.
- **Camdenton, Missouri**, which uses its access adjacent to the Lake of the Ozarks to host many fishing tournaments and other lake activities.
- **Logan, Utah**, in the Cache Valley, which novelist Thomas Wolfe called, "The most lovely and enchanted valley I have ever seen, a valley that makes all that has gone before fade as nothing."
- **Lake Placid, New York**, with its pristine mountains, lakes and streams. Having hosted two Winter Olympics (1932 and 1980), Lake Placid shares this distinction with only two other communities: Innsbruck, Austria, and St. Moritz, Switzerland. It draws more than 1.8 million visitors annually.

This list goes on and on—and could include your town, if it is on a major river or lake that attracts boaters, campers and other recreation enthusiasts or if it has forests or mountains that are not only beautiful to view and explore but also that lure tourists for skiing, hiking, climbing and camping.

Vail, Colorado: Banking on Its Beauty

Pete Seibert returned from World War II with a dream of creating a European skiing experience in the United States. For years Seibert searched for the ideal spot, eventually finding a peak called No-Name Mountain just over Colorado's Vail Pass.

It wasn't until 1962 that all of the legal and financial details were worked out and Seibert could begin construction of Vail's first ski resort. At the time, Vail consisted of four houses, one telephone, and virtually no other modern amenities (except for a flush toilet or two). The University of Denver's ski coach called the effort futile, saying, "Vail is too flat to ever be a successful ski mountain."

Seibert used such comments to turn lemons into lemonade. He promoted his new resort, which opened with three lifts, as a great place for beginner skiers and their families. The early visitors were ski bums. But soon others began flocking to the friendly slopes with the $8 per-day lift tickets; by 1969 Vail was the most popular resort in Colorado. When Interstate 70 was built near Vail in the early 1970s, access to the rapidly growing town improved and ever since Vail has been on an upswing as a bustling, year-round outdoor recreation town.

Many other communities aren't blessed to have the same type of natural resources. But until Pete Siebert came along, Vail was about as no-name as the mountain that loomed nearby.

Many towns are situated in beautiful areas or have attractive climates—but they don't draw tourists. At the same time, a town 10 or 20 miles down the road prospers while enjoying the same natural surroundings and attractions. Why the difference? Because the first town likely doesn't have a plan for attracting visitors, isn't set up to accommodate tourists or doesn't have a vision for how it can use its resources. Or perhaps it has the vision but doesn't know how to carry it out. Regardless, the town blessed with great natural resources and with the vision to use those resources to boost its economy can make a name for itself.

Man-made resources such as lakes, parks and recreation areas.
Communities not situated by forests, mountains, lakes or rivers can still attract visitors and pump up their income through their own resourcefulness. Countless communities have benefited from creating man-made lakes, parks and recreation areas, often around existing natural resources. Such resources

make the town more attractive and benefit residents and visitors alike. The best use of such man-made resources complements and enhances the environment, rather than destroys it.

For example, Crossville, Tennessee, a town of only 8,981, has turned itself into the "Golf Capital of Tennessee." Using its natural beauty as a backdrop, Crossville has encouraged world-renowned golf course designers such as Jack Nicklaus to build 11 golf courses nearby, giving the town the distinction of having the most golf courses per capita in the world. Crossville draws thousands of golfers from near and far to take advantage of its many challenging courses.

Other man-made resources that can enhance a community—but are sometimes taken for granted—include highway and railway systems and infrastructure. At the Texas junction of I-35 West and I-35 East, just north of Waco, sits Hillsboro, Texas. Hillsboro's strategic location is home to a 100-plus store outlet shopping center and more than 200 antique dealers. The Hillsboro Chamber of Commerce/Convention and Visitors Bureau reports that its retail establishments draw shoppers from at least a 100-mile radius.

Local celebrities (either living or dead). Americans are fascinated with fame and fortune. Those who have "made it big" provide an endless array of media coverage and scrutiny. The media may exploit celebrities, but their hometowns or current towns usually treat them with kindness and pride (especially the smaller towns). Celebrities act as attention-getters for your town. They can put you on the map for curiosity-seekers and fans, can make your town a stopping-off point on trips and vacations or spur a weekend visit.

Carl Sandburg, the Pulitzer Prize winning poet, author and historian, was born and raised in Galesburg, Illinois. That town has preserved Sandburg's boyhood home and opened it as a tourist attraction. Hendersonville, North Carolina, also lays claim to Sandburg, if not as a native son, then as a longtime resident. His home in Hendersonville and his farm outside of town are well-visited sites.

Hannibal, Missouri, where the writer Mark Twain grew up, offers one of the best examples of a town that has capitalized upon a local celebrity. Hannibal has bookstores, gift shops, museums, theaters, monuments and emporiums celebrating the life of Twain and the characters he created: Huckleberry Finn, Tom Sawyer and Becky Thatcher, among others. Hannibal hosts National Tom Sawyer Days each summer; the Samuel L. Clemens Arts & Crafts Festival; and numerous other festivals, rodeos, and events throughout the year. In celebrating its most famous son, Hannibal not only perpetuates Twain's colorful and talented life but also has created hundreds of jobs and pumped millions of dollars into the community.

Towns like Tupelo, Mississippi (Elvis Presley's birthplace); Liberal, Kansas (home of Dorothy's Wizard of Oz House); and Greenville, Tennessee (birthplace of Davy Crockett and the 17th U. S. President, Andrew Johnson) all have used their real and invented celebrities to their advantage. Tupelo, for one, attracts more than 100,000 people each year to see the simple house where Elvis was born.

From Podunk to Pennsylvania Avenue

Of the 17 U.S. presidents who served in the 20th century—beginning with Theodore Roosevelt and ending with Bill Clinton—12 were born in small towns. Here's the list of those presidents, their years in office, and the towns they were born or raised in, with the population from the 2000 census:

Woodrow Wilson, 1913–1921—Staunton, Virginia (population 23,853)

Warren G. Harding, 1921–1923—Corsica, Ohio (a town that no longer exists) and raised in Caledonia, Ohio (population 578)

Calvin Coolidge, 1923–1929—Plymouth, Vermont (population 555)

Herbert Hoover, 1929–1933—West Branch, Iowa (population 2,188); grew up in Newburg, Oregon (population 18,064)

Franklin D. Roosevelt, 1933–1945—Hyde Park, New York (population 20,851)

Harry S Truman, 1945–1953—Lamar, Missouri (population 4,425)

Dwight D. Eisenhower, 1953–1961—Denison, Texas (population 22,773); grew up in Abilene, Kansas (population 6,543)

Lyndon B. Johnson, 1963–1969—Stonewall, Texas (population 469); raised in Johnson City, Texas (population 1,191)

Jimmy Carter, 1977–1981—Plains, Georgia (population 637)

Ronald Reagan, 1981–1989—Tampico, Illinois (population 772); raised in Dixon, Illinois (population 15,941)

George Bush, 1989–1993—Milton, Massachusetts (population 26,062)

Bill Clinton, 1993–2001—Hope, Arkansas (population 10,616); grew up in Hot Springs, Arkansas (population 35,750)

Local flavor. This is the essence of your town—its greatest strength or attribute or what distinguishes it from other towns. Think for a moment of a chili contest. You can have 10 different varieties that look essentially the same, but each cook has used slightly different ingredients. Some cooks used hamburger, some used sausage, some didn't include any meat; some entries have beans and peppers, and others have neither. All have different seasonings, making each chili a creation with a distinct flavor.

So it is with towns. A multitude of "flavors" go into any town, and together they blend to create a flavor that can draw others to the community. If beauty is in the eye of the beholder, taste is in the preferences and interests of the visitor (and potential resident).

What ingredients give a town its distinctive flavor? Review the following list and consider which items, if any, are part of your town's strengths. You might have additional ones as well:

- Climate
- Schools
- Colleges and universities
- Churches
- Native animals or fish
- Historical events (battles, speeches and so on)
- Location within the state and United States
- Locally manufactured products
- Locally produced agricultural products
- Distinct customs and cultures (such as with Native Americans, Amish, Mennonites)
- Festivals and celebrations

What is your town known for? Perhaps it is home to a nationally known producer of salad dressings and sauces, as is Sandpoint, Idaho (Litehouse Dressings), or maybe it can lay claim to presidential fame as does Paragould, Arkansas (from where orders of Oinky's Ribs were sent regularly to the Clinton White House). Perhaps it is home to a custom-built furniture shop known for its fine design and workmanship, such as C.H. Becksvoort in New Gloucester, Maine. Maybe you live in a cultural center, such as Berlin, Ohio, home of an educational and heritage center for the Amish and Mennonite communities. Or perhaps you live near the site of a famous Civil War battle, such as Manassas, Virginia. Or maybe it's a battle of less historical significance but can still be used for reenactments, such as Chickasaw Bluffs and Snyder's Mill, located in Warren County, Mississippi; or the Demonstration on Dalton in Dalton, Georgia.

Similarly, the Flathead Valley Area, Montana (Kalispell, Whitefish and Bigfork); Deer Isle and Blue Hill, Maine; and Easton, Maryland, have all leveraged their heritage by evolving into artists' colonies. The towns attract local artists, which draw more tourists, and so on. The circle of success continues, growing ever bigger. In the case of Flathead Valley, it boasts more than 2,000 artists and craftsmen and one of the highest concentrations of bronze-casting foundries in the nation.

Both Beaufort, South Carolina, and Park City, Utah, have extensive performing arts programs that run through spring and summer. While both programs began primarily as local events, they have achieved a regional following, bringing in thousands of tourists.

Your town doesn't have to be located in a certain type of area, or be home to a certain type of product or event, to capitalize on its local flavor. In keeping with the chili analogy, remember that not everyone likes hot and spicy chili; some are more satisfied by a mild, rich-flavored dish. So rather than making your town into something it's not, invest your time and resources wisely by drawing out all the natural flavor that already resides in your town—and making that flavor known beyond your town limits. (See Appendix B for examples of towns that excel in various areas of local flavor.)

Local "brain bank." For a town to prosper, its "brain bank" must be in good standing and have plenty in reserve. A community has a rich brain bank when it has a solid core of bright people who are committed to the community's welfare. Those people can be young or old and ideally should come from different backgrounds and work experiences.

Diversity of experience and thought is not only good for a community, it is an indicator of health. Towns afraid of expressing differences of opinion, or always looking to the same few people to determine their paths, are destined for trouble. Towns that welcome differing opinions and that fairly consider those opinions for their value to the community are more likely to thrive. Frank Tamberrino, president of The Maury Alliance in Columbia, Tennessee, probably said it best: "Adversity brings lively debates in commission meetings and in the local media." The key to success is to set the debate aside once the decision is made, to come together and to move on to carrying out the decision and solving the next problem.

Here's how to ensure your town has a rich brain bank upon which to draw:

1. Retain the Current Brain Bank. One of the primary struggles of small towns is raising sons and daughters only to see the brightest go off to college and return only for holiday visits. It's natural for young people to want to broaden their horizons, and other good opportunities present themselves. But when the vast majority of high school graduates leave town, never to return, it's a warning signal that the town is beginning to die.

Almost half of Iowa's counties lost population during the 1990s, and the state has come up with a plan to retain people. The plan addresses the problem on three fronts. First, Governor Tom Vilsack wants to keep young Iowans from moving away in the first place. With more than 60 percent of Iowa college grads moving away, the state maintains a Web site (www.smartcareer move.com) that lists more than 1,500 professional and technical job openings in the state. Second, to bring back Iowans, the state has launched a direct mail campaign to reach the hundreds of thousands of Iowa grads who no longer live there. Third, to attract skilled immigrants, Vilsack has established "New Iowa" grants to help cities lure people from around the globe to make their home in Iowa.

Robinson, Illinois: Hatching Good Ideas

Robinson, a town of 6,822 in the southeastern part of Illinois, has created a business incubator project to develop and support entrepreneurs. The non-profit incubator, established through public and private entities, is staffed with people who help local entrepreneurs develop their ideas and the business skills they need to succeed. The town not only helps hatch the ideas but also has formed focus groups to develop a strategic plan to attract and retain business. In addition, the groups present business opportunities to graduates of the incubator in an attempt to retain them.

Norma Carder, head of the Crawford County Development Association, says, "The incubator has been very positive and is an economic development tool grown from the inside out. Sixty to 70 percent of Crawford County's growth has come from within. When local people take ownership of an idea or project, they are much more committed."

2. Reconnect with Former Residents. When people move away, they often retain a connection to the town through family and friends or perhaps through teachers and coaches they had in school. By keeping these connections alive, especially within the business community, good things can happen for the town as its former residents gain experience and connections in the outside world. A former resident can directly lend his or her hand to a project or be the bridge between the town and an outside agency or company that can partner with the town.

Here are a few examples of what can happen through maintaining connections:

- David Samuel grew up in Waterville, Maine, and during high school and college was a DJ for local dances. When he graduated from MIT, Samuel set up a DJ company on the Internet named Spinner.com. Spinner was a huge success; when Samuel sold the company to America Online, he pocketed tens of millions of dollars. The entrepreneur hasn't forgotten his hometown; he returns often and recently donated a media lab to his high school.

- Larry Sur climbed the corporate ladder to the top of Schneider Logistics, one of the leading international logistics companies. When he retired, he set up a consulting company. One of his first clients was his hometown, Effingham, Illinois, which through Sur's discounted billing was able to do a study on why it was an ideal national distribution location. As a result of the study, several national companies located there.

- Larry Smith, a sports anchor for Cable News Network, grew up in Mattoon, Illinois. He holds an annual fundraising event to award more than $25,000 in scholarships to local high school students.

- Bart Holaday, a former venture capitalist, served as managing partner and head of a private equity group in Chicago. Before retiring in 2000, Holaday decided to help his home state of North Dakota by establishing The Dakota Foundation. He used an entrepreneurial, venture-based approach with the foundation, which focuses on various humanitarian and economic development issues, including helping the aging population by converting old school houses into senior centers.

3. Make New Connections. Maintaining connections with former residents is one way to network. You can also network with people or organizations with whom you formerly had *no* connection. This can open the door to accessing state and federal funding.

Most local projects, especially larger ones, can only be accomplished through a combined effort on the local front, both public and private, and with state and national financial assistance. Whether it's a road improvement project, an infrastructure upgrade to a water or sewer system or a completely new project, a project typically has to be pushed from the local level. The state or national politicians don't usually show up saying, "How would you like a new lake or a new water system?" Funding for such projects is limited and requires the combined efforts of many.

West Branch, Michigan, is a town of 2,000 in sparsely populated northeast Michigan, surrounded by woods and lakes. Most of the neighboring towns haven't changed much in the past 20 or so years. Their inaction has allowed West Branch to surge ahead. It has built the region's only mall and developed a bustling commercial district and renowned regional medical center. "West Branch has done an impressive job developing itself," says Linda Barnes, a regional development coordinator and director of a neighboring economic development group. "They're extremely progressive. They don't impose the limits on themselves that I see in other communities. They're ahead of the rest of us."

Indeed, by working together as a community, West Branch has landed more than $3 million in outside public grants for art, music and sports facilities, in addition to upgrading its basic infrastructure.

Beating Bureaucracies

I had my first experience with networking for funds in the early 1990s. My company had been assisting our community in developing an industrial park to recruit new businesses. However, railroad tracks hindered access to that part of town. People going to and from work and the businesses themselves found the heavily used tracks an inconvenience. Most important, the tracks represented a major safety concern for accessing fire and ambulance service in an emergency.

A local coalition from the public and private sectors prepared a plan, secured an audience with the governor and successfully funded the $13 million overpass project from state, federal and local sources. Today, you can travel over or under those tracks without having to wait for a train. We have used this same strategy in other cities to assist in funding projects that would be impossible to accomplish solely from local sources.

Of course, networking doesn't have to be limited to people or agencies. Town-to-town networking can give rise to relationships and partnerships that can benefit both parties. Remember John Nash's Equilibrium Theory, outlined in Chapter 1, wherein rivals could coexist and even benefit one another? This win-win paradigm is played out as small towns partner together on projects. One town may provide the brains, while the other provides the brawn, yet the result is mutually beneficial.

Following are examples of communities that have marshaled their resources for multi-community projects. In effect, they have expanded the pie rather than fighting one another for a larger slice of the pie.

- **Door County, Wisconsin,** sits on a peninsula that separates Green Bay and Lake Michigan. It is a series of small towns that alone wouldn't have the resources to promote themselves. But, by billing themselves collectively as Door County, they have established themselves as one of the premier recreational spots in the Midwest. For years Door County has attracted creative and artistic people, with more than 100 full-time artists making their homes in the area. Two theaters also operate during the summer months.
- **The San Juan Islands, Washington,** a chain of small islands, promotes its artists and small businesses together, rather than having each individual island trying to do it all.
- The areas surrounding **Brunswick, Georgia,** also work together in promoting tourism. This area comprises Brunswick and the Golden Isles of St. Simons Island, Sea Island, Little St. Simons Island and Jekyll Island. The tourism group operates a welcome center and two visitors' centers.
- **The Amana Colonies,** a group of small towns in southeast Iowa, have banded together to promote the region's historic, unique heritage. By working together, the colonies are able to host, every third year, the Farm Progress Show, the Midwest's largest farm show.

Key #4: Raise Up Strong Leaders

L eaders come in all shapes and sizes and from all walks of life. They are sometimes elected; sometimes they step forth when the situation demands it. Some are born to lead, while others are made to lead by being the right person in the right place at the right time. And some provide leadership for a minute, an hour or a day, and are forever remembered afterward for that brief moment.

In small towns, leadership does not just come from the mayor, the town council, the town attorney or manager or the chamber of commerce. People in all sectors—government, business, education, healthcare, religious, service, private—have not only the opportunity but also the responsibility to play a leadership role in their area of expertise. How effectively people from these sectors play those roles helps determine the town's growth and health. In many small towns, it's not unusual for the leaders who step forward to wear several hats. In Chipley, Florida, for example, the mayor is also the executive director of the chamber of commerce and the economic developer. Pinckneyville, Illinois, has one of the more unusual combinations: The full-time police chief is also the city's part-time economic developer.

Many Are Called

The lazy view of leadership is that someone else needs to do it, and that only few are called to lead. This is faulty thinking, as Peter Senge points out in Russ S. Moxley's book, *Leadership and Spirit* (Jossey-Bass, 1999): "One reason that the myth of the great leader is so appealing is that it absolves us of the responsibility for developing leadership capabilities more broadly," Senge points out. "A perceived need for leadership… can be met by developing leadership capabilities through the organization…, not just by relying on a hero leader… leadership is inevitably collective."

Indeed, singular leadership mocks the democratic way of life. To rely on one or a few leaders—whether within a school, a business, an organization or the town government—is to fire up only one of four jet engines, relying on that one to get you safely to your destination. This is both unnecessary and dangerous. If the government is truly "of the people, by the people and for the people," then *the people* ought to get involved. Great leaders know this, so they surround themselves with people who have wisdom and strengths in all the areas that they govern. They consult with these people, trust them and are guided by them.

Leadership is traditionally understood to be reserved for a few special seats, but in reality it is everywhere—or it can be. In towns that operate effectively, continuing to grow and prosper, true leadership is spread among a multitude of people. True leadership has no respect for age, gender, socioeconomic background, education, position, title or experience. It can come from 95-year-old men and women who have ideas to improve the economy, based on principles that are older than they are. It can come from mothers who spend their days transporting children, changing diapers and attending parent-teacher meetings. It can come from school children who have a great idea for their school, for a town festival or for a new park. It can come from immigrants who barely know English but know how to improve workplace efficiency. It can come from anywhere and everywhere. Those in the traditional seats of leadership not only know this, they live and breathe it.

No single hero will ride into your town on a white horse and save your community from calamity. There are only the people of your town—your friends and neighbors; your merchants and businesspeople; your pastors, priests and rabbis; your firefighters and police force; your bankers and insurance agents; your doctors, lawyers, teachers and administrators; your clerks and assistants; your managers and machinists; your town council and chamber of commerce; your mayor, village attorney and city manager. Collectively, these people have a wealth of wisdom and experience. Collectively, they have high ideals, dreams and visions. Together, they hold the future of your town in their hands. As do you.

9 Traits of Strong Local Leadership

Although true leadership should be a shared commitment among many people, a community tends to mirror the vision, passion and commitment found within its local government. You can see this trickle-down effect in business and sports, where employees often take on the attitude of the company executives and where athletes often reflect, in their play, their coach's or manager's outlook and personality.

Tupelo, Mississippi: Spreading the News

In 1934, when George McLean bought the bankrupt weekly newspaper in Tupelo, Mississippi, he didn't just want to resurrect a newspaper: He wanted to resuscitate a town. His life goal, in his own words, was to "serve God and mankind," and he set about doing that in Tupelo.

McLean believed that Tupelo's future lay in the area around the town as much as within the town, that the only way to make progress was to elevate the poorest residents and that local citizens needed to invest their own time and money to raise the quality of life for everyone in Tupelo.

McLean's first project was rather modest. He convinced 16 other local businesspeople to buy a bull, which was used to inseminate dairy cows at $5 per cow. This helped develop a small dairy base in the county and provided many of the poorer local farmers with a steady monthly cash flow from milk. Then, in 1948, McLean and a group of business leaders raised $25,000 from 151 local businesses and formed the Community Development Foundation. This organization became the linchpin for bettering the life of virtually all citizens in Tupelo and surrounding Lee County.

McLean actively promoted the efforts to attract new industry in his newspaper, which he transformed from a weekly to a highly successful independent daily. He also pushed for equal footing for all races; in 1965, when the local schools desegregated, they did so without incident. McLean studied how northern Alabama developed its economy and brought some of that region's more innovative techniques to Lee County. In 1972 he and his wife established a community charitable foundation called CREATE (Christian, Research, Education, Action, Technical Enterprise). Through this foundation, the town was able to purchase ownership of the newspaper when McLean died in 1983, thus carrying on his goals and projects.

McLean's efforts helped bring in new industry and diversify the economy of the entire region. Today, Lee County is the second wealthiest county in Mississippi and hosts more than 200 highly diversified manufacturers—amazing when you consider Tupelo is in a largely rural region. This county has only 72,000 residents—and 52,000 jobs.

Garden City, Kansas: Tested by Fire

Christmas Day is normally a time for family, reflection, thankfulness, and peace. But December 25, 2000, ended anyway but peacefully in Garden City, Kansas. That's the day a fire ravaged one of the two meatpacking plants in Garden City, a town of 30,000 located in the plains of western Kansas. The ConAgra plant's closing put 2,300 people—more than 10 percent of the town's workforce—out of work overnight.

The town had previously instituted a Leadership Garden City program and changed its leadership development focus from people with connections to people with passion. That passion was displayed as town leaders responded to the disaster. They made sure state unemployment funds were available, counseled displaced workers on how to receive their benefits, made extra social services available, cut the city budget in anticipation of reduced revenue (ConAgra's annual payroll was $43 million), and worked out a set of incentives to encourage ConAgra to reopen its plant.

The plant closing caused unemployment to soar from its normal three to four percent to nearly 12 percent. But within a year of the fire, unemployment had dropped to 5.8 percent, though few unemployed workers moved to find work elsewhere. Expansion in retail, health services, social services and support industries (such as warehousing and trucking) helped offset the loss of the meatpacking plant. Although the plant is not expected to reopen, Garden City has shown its resiliency and demonstrated the importance of capable leadership in coming back from the disaster.

For example, the great run of the Chicago Bulls in the 1990s was certainly fueled by Michael Jordan and his talented teammates, including Scottie Pippen, but it was masterminded and guided by Phil Jackson, one of the most successful coaches in National Basketball Association history. Sure, any coach would drool to have the exquisite talents of Jordan and his teammates, but the task was not as easy as it looked. After all, every sport has had teams with exceptional talent that could never put it together to win a championship.

The Chicago Bulls won six championships in eight years, and they did it without a dominant center or an all-star point guard, the typical requisites of champions. They did it without the rest of the team sitting around waiting for Michael Jordan to create something, as many teams with a superstar do. And they did it without the common bickering and cliques that form on teams with a superstar. As Jackson says in his book, *Sacred Hoops* (Hyperion, 1995), "The real reason the Bulls won… was that we plugged in to the power of *oneness* instead of the power of one man, and transcended the divisive forces of the ego that have crippled far more gifted teams." It was Jackson who engineered the cohesiveness, teamwork and system that allowed the Bulls to accomplish one of the greatest runs in sports history.

In a similar fashion, each town resident has partial responsibility for the town's progress and success. How private citizens interact with local government can determine the fate of the town. A successful town raises up leaders from various sectors, empowering "people with passion," and giving each citizen a voice. It must invite and consider differences of opinion, have a local government that remains open and flexible and encourage significant interaction with town residents. Specifically, the best town leaders do the following:

1. Create a positive and open working environment and have can-do attitudes. A positive environment sets the stage for good things to happen and for government, business and other sectors to work well together. When a town encourages open discussion and operates with a can-do attitude, it allows the other key traits to flourish. For the business and private sectors, a positive environment facilitates a communal atmosphere in which cooperation and problem-solving become prominent—all focused on what's best for the community.

2. Have a strong vision for the community. A strong vision goes hand in hand with a positive environment—and which comes first is a chicken-or-egg question. A positive environment allows for town leaders to play their part in creating a vision for the town, and having and pursuing such a vision reinforces an open working environment and a can-do attitude.

Towns without vision are likely in trouble or headed for it. *Double* vision—when different entities don't see eye to eye and have conflicting goals that affect the community—is nearly as bad as *no* vision. When local government and the business community are continually at odds with each other, no one wins. It is neither unusual nor harmful to have some tension and conflict, some checks and balances, between government and business. But for the town to move forward, those two entities need to share the same vision.

In 1987 Coeur d'Alene, Idaho, formed its Jobs Plus Economic Development Group and, in Bob Potter, found someone who shared its vision for continued growth. Potter, a former vice president of sales for AT&T who emerged from retirement to run the group, has scored impressive successes. He has attracted 74 companies to the region—representing 3,780 jobs and $85 million in payroll—and has helped garner $340 million in capital investment.

3. Promote teamwork among the various sectors and government.

When a town operates in a positive, open environment and shares a commitment to the same overall vision, the result is a cohesive, effective effort among all sectors and individuals. The town that achieves real teamwork, with each sector playing its role and with all sectors sharing the same vision for the town's health and growth, is the one that will reap success.

The movie *Hoosiers* portrays this concept vividly (and appropriately). It recounts the story of a high school basketball team from Milan, Indiana (population: 1,816), which beats a big-city team in the Indiana State Finals. The small-town team struggles early in the season because its players are selfish and uncommitted. When the coach demands selflessness and commitment—and dares them to believe in themselves and have a great vision—the boys become an unstoppable, winning team. The result—based on a true story—is a highly unlikely state championship and a testimony to the heights to which teamwork can take an underdog and a small town. The real-life event has attained legendary status in Indiana, which has long revered basketball.

The same principles of teamwork, commitment, belief and vision work just as well for small towns trying to win their own version of a championship by achieving economic growth and revitalization. It is not only acceptable but also necessary that each sector has its own goals. Each sector brings strength and purpose to the town and has its own role to play in the town's health. Those goals must mesh together, however, to create a vibrant, valuable mosaic for the town.

A couple of examples of teamwork pop to mind. Both are related to natural disasters, which have a way of focusing a town's efforts on solving a major problem. When Mount St. Helens exploded in 1980, Moses Lake, Washington, woke up one morning to find six inches of volcanic ash covering every square inch of the town. The citizens quickly rallied together and shoveled themselves back into a normal existence. Similarly, the Mississippi River Flood of 1993 demonstrated the teamwork and compassion of many small towns in Minnesota, Wisconsin, Iowa, Illinois and Missouri, as townspeople along the river fought to save levees and sandbag their communities.

Buffalo County, Nebraska: Teaming Up to Bend Trends

In the early 1990s, the citizens of Buffalo County, Nebraska, began voicing concerns about disturbing trends they saw in domestic violence, teen pregnancies, suicide rates and senior citizens' healthcare. People from Kearney (the county seat) and other towns in this county of 41,000 began discussing how they might turn around some of these negatives. They formed the Buffalo County Community Health Partners as part of a Trendbending Initiative.

The partners undertook a countywide assessment in 1994 and identified 15 priorities to address. Within seven years, community volunteers had worked together to achieve more than half of those priorities, including the creation of an Alzheimer treatment center; an increase in the number of assisted living units available to seniors; and a reduction in domestic violence incidents, teen pregnancies and suicides. The goals achieved in the first Trendbending Initiative were accomplished with only $290,713 in grants from various entities.

The group continues to meet and has drafted an action plan through 2006. The new priorities include reducing lead levels in children, improving access to healthcare for the Hispanic population, increasing the number of adequate affordable housing units and expanding public transportation.

4. Keep the right priorities in mind when making decisions. For the local government, "right priorities" means remembering that it exists to serve the community. The community's welfare is paramount; the government should base all of its decisions on how the outcomes of those decisions will positively affect the community's welfare.

This can become a sticking point for some towns, especially those in which the government and business sectors are not on the same page. In such cases, the government might *assume* it knows what is best for the community and push for legislation and growth in areas that oppose what the business community has in mind. The lesson here is that you can't serve your community very well if you don't know the goals and desires of the people within it. Part of being able to keep the right priorities is to effectively communicate with business and private sectors. No government can effectively serve its community if it doesn't share the vision of its people.

5. Hear the concerns of citizens, and remain open to criticism. The best small-town governments cultivate passion and conviction among town residents. They bring people from the various sectors together and encourage them to share their views on present paths and future direction. When passion and conviction fuse with knowledge, experience and vision, the future of a town is bright. A wise local government orchestrates this fusion and acknowledges that passion and conviction know no boundaries in terms of race, age, gender or socioeconomic standing. Likewise, a wise government knows that knowledge and experience alone are lifeless without passion and conviction.

One sign of an unhealthy town is when concerns are left unspoken or fall on deaf ears because the local government remains set in its ways and has a history of unwillingness to heed its citizens. In certain respects the relationship between a government and its citizens resembles that of a marriage: When communication breaks down, or when one side feels the other is not listening, the relationship is damaged. Consequences for a town include missed opportunities; lack of growth; a negative, antagonistic outlook; and a low morale that hangs heavy on the town and impedes positive momentum.

An unhealthy relationship doesn't necessarily begin and end with the local government's lack of ability to listen or care. Perhaps the government has steeled itself to feedback from its citizens because, in effect, "a few bad apples have spoiled the bunch." That is, a few cranks or chronic complainers have caused a reflexive action to take place among government officials. They begin to view *all* residents as cranks and complainers and thus erect an invisible but real wall between government and its citizens.

Strong leaders recognize that new ideas can be difficult for many in a community to accept. New ideas might be met with counter arguments such as, "We've always done it that way," "That will never work here," "What if it fails?" and "Someone (other than me) might benefit from this." And while it is usually easier to rally support *against* something, towns will continue in the same pattern they are presently in if the new ideas aren't tried. Visionary leaders take to heart the saying, "The biggest risk is not taking one."

6. Do not shy away from challenges or problems. There are many ways to approach problems and challenges. Denial is a tantalizingly strong option; it is easy to simply ignore difficulty, because the specter of hard work and the risk of failure loom too large. Self-promotion is another approach: As problems arise, each faction and sector affected by the problem carves out its own solution, based on its own self-interest (and often to the detriment of the other factions and sectors).

Eufaula, Alabama: Strategic Plan Takes Flight

Eufaula, Alabama, sits on the banks of bass-filled Lake Eufaula and adjacent to the 11,000-acre Eufaula National Wildlife Refuge. More than 300 species of birds spend part of the year there, along with deer, bobcats, foxes and many other mammals.

The 13,908 citizens of Eufaula decided to use the abundant natural resources to improve their economy and spur job growth while adhering to responsible conservation methods. The idea had taken root several years earlier when Eufaula's golf courses earned a special designation from Audubon International for conserving water and preserving habitat for wildlife. This award led to new initiatives, resulting in Audubon International naming the town the first "Audubon Cooperative Sanctuary" city in the United States.

Approximately 1,000 citizens met during a 17-month period to develop the "Eufaula 2020" Strategic Plan, presented to the city council in the fall of 2002. A key part of the plan is that the city, in planning for and acting on the issues, takes into account the impact upon the environment. Mayor Jay Jaxon, Jr., says, "We're trying to get everybody in the community to try to establish what kind of community we want to be, then develop a strategy for how to get there." He plans on holding quarterly meetings to track the progress of the town's 20-year plan.

Finger-pointing is another time-honored tradition. Finger-pointers are quick to identify the source of the problem (which is never them) and the size of the problem and note that they never would have had to face the problem were it not for the guilty parties who bungled the whole deal. The "fret or freeze" approaches are at extreme ends of the reaction pole but have the same results. You can fret, worry, wring your hands and talk incessantly about the problem, expending great energy on it and never accomplishing anything. Or you can freeze in terror, overwhelmed by the immensity of the problem and its implications.

The effective approach to problems—and the deceivingly simplistic explanation—is to be a problem solver. A problem solver acknowledges challenges, brings together those who can help solve the problem and invests energy in identifying—sometimes even creating—solutions.

The 4,736 residents of Clintonville, Wisconsin, did not back away from the challenge presented in the aftermath of the 9/11 terrorist attacks in New York

City. The town, located 52 miles west of Green Bay, is known as Truck City because it is home to the Seagrave Fire Apparatus Plant. With 360 employees, Seagrave is by far the largest employer in the town—and the chief supplier of ladders, pumpers and engines for the New York City Fire Department.

When New York City placed an order for 54 replacement fire trucks, the manufacturer hired additional workers and worked double shifts to deliver the first truck in record time. In addition, Seagrave donated a $350,000 custom pumper to the city on behalf of its employees.

7. Make decisions based on the community's long-term welfare.
The most effective problem solvers always remember the long-term welfare of the community. They take into account the vision for the community; its strengths, resources and advantages; the industries and workforces within a town; and what will keep all those areas vibrant and healthy. The best solutions are long-lasting. Often, short-term answers can undermine a community's long-term health or success.

The State of Utah, in cooperation with Weber State University, provides a good example of working toward a long-term vision for its people. Utah began Utah Smart Sites, an initiative dedicated to providing technology-based jobs in rural Utah through Internet use. The state initially provided 15 scholarships to train people from rural areas of the state to become medical coding specialists. Already committed is AviaCode, a company that delivers online medical coding services for healthcare providers. It plans to hire 100 medical coding specialists at an average rate of $15 per hour—which is 32 percent more than the average made by a non-farm wage earner.

8. Are willing to share leadership and the "spoils." In a competitive and capitalistic society most people focus on getting the biggest piece of pie possible. They look out for themselves first and foremost, at least in terms of business and profits. In contrast, effective leaders favor a strategy that benefits everyone. The most astute business leaders understand that such a strategy is not only in *the town's* best interests but in *their* best interests as well.

Being willing to share leadership will expand a town's future by expanding current businesses, bringing in new industries and generating revenue through town festivals and other special events. In short, it spreads the wealth around, bringing in more capital and more jobs and potentially creating the need for new housing, which is a boon to construction companies and related service companies. That's how expansion works: One area of growth causes another area to grow, which affects another area, and so on. Pretty soon the pie is larger for everyone. Rather than fighting for your own small piece—and eyeing others with suspicion lest they sneak in and steal it—you can sit down and enjoy a feast with your fellow citizens.

Such expansion rarely comes easily or quickly, and it isn't always easy to convince others that expansion is a realistic, or even the best, route. Many are used to scratching and scraping for what they can get and view any other approach with suspicion. Town leaders need to be able to share a vision with the business community and articulate how the entire town can expand its pie to the benefit of all.

9. Develop leaders for the future. Town leaders should aim to excel at grooming people to replace them. Consider the example of a church that springs to life in a small town; its pastors, leaders and congregation are all young adults with enthusiasm and a desire to serve the community. As the church ages, some new members join, but by and large they are about the same age as the majority of the congregation—middle-aged by now. They still are enthusiastic and still serve the community in a variety of ways, but they are not retaining younger members. By the time the church reaches old age, its congregation has slowed considerably and its outreach has diminished. The congregation sees no young adults within its ranks to take up the charge, to pick up where they left off. So the church dwindles and dies off as its members pass away.

Belvidere, Illinois: An Enterprising Way of Doing Business

Like many rural communities, Belvidere, Illinois, has an Enterprise Zone. Typically, an Enterprise Zone is established to entice new industry by offering financial incentives, such as a property tax abatement for a limited number of years, sales tax relief on building a new plant and various tax credits based upon job creation (See Chapter 7: Encourage an Entrepreneurial Approach).

Belvidere has given its Enterprise Zone an interesting twist. If an original company (one recruited into the zone) recruits one of its suppliers to the community within five years, it receives additional property tax abatement for up to eight years on a sliding scale. Several companies are seriously considering Belvidere because of this unique incentive.

So it is with small towns that don't look to the future. Without the passing of the leadership torch, the town itself will be like the church—tired, feeble, unable to continue. Instead, involve young adults in leadership roles within your town. Give them a taste of responsibility. Let them experience ownership and commitment and see that they can make a difference.

It's common for young adults to yearn to make a difference in the world, and small towns are an ideal venue for them. In small towns individual voices can still be heard, a sense of community is still prevalent and prominent and people can still see the results of their efforts—more so than in big cities. Examples of towns that have formalized programs for their residents, including students and young adults, are:

- **Clanton, Alabama:** The Chilton County Chamber of Commerce that serves Clanton runs an annual Leadership Course from September through May (one full day per month) on subjects such as county history, economic development, education, public safety and local government. The course is designed to prepare local citizens to assume positions of leadership within the county.

- **Hammond, Louisiana:** The Hammond Youth Development Committee was formed in 2000 as part of the city's strategic plan to give a voice to local teens. As part of this initiative, a local teen newspaper is published monthly within the local newspaper.

- **Colville, Washington:** The Colville Youth Commission was founded to make recommendations to the city for the purpose of improving the quality of life for Colville-area youths.

- **Galesburg, Illinois:** Galesburg is the home to the Knox County Teen Court, a volunteer organization established to give youth offenders a chance to clear arrests from their permanent records by performing community service. The offenders agree to accept their sentences as given by a jury of peers—that is, other teens. Teen Court also gives teens a chance to participate in the judicial process.

- **Hastings, Michigan:** The local chamber of commerce offers a program called Leadership Barry County that is designed to enhance leadership skills for individual growth, organizational improvement and increased community effectiveness. The objectives of the program are for the participants to gain knowledge and understanding of the community, learn how to affect public policy and comprehend political and financial structures within the community.

Reverend Martin Luther King., Jr., once exhorted his congregation with these words: "I want you to be first in love. I want you to be first in moral excellence. I want you to be first in generosity. If you want to be important, wonderful. If you want to be great, wonderful. But recognize that he who is greatest among you shall be your servant."

King hit it on the head: True leadership is about serving. A leader serves the town by sacrificing what's good for just one person or group to attain the best for the entire community.

LEAVENWORTH, WASHINGTON

Front Street, Leavenworth, circa 1950s—not very distinguishable from thousands of other small towns. (Photograph courtesy of Leavenworth Chamber of Commerce from *Miracle Town*)

Front Street, Leavenworth, as it is today—distinct in its Bavarian motif. (Photograph courtesy of Robert Smith, Leavenworth, Washington)

BRANSON, MISSOURI

Presleys' Country Jubilee—the first music show to perform on the strip in Branson. (Photograph courtesy of Presleys', Inc.)

Branson's first theatre, Jim Owen's Hillbilly Theatre, sparked an idea for the town—an idea that transformed Branson into a music center that brings more than 7 million visitors annually. (Photograph courtesy of Townsend Godsey, copyright Manta Ray Publishing)

EFFINGHAM, ILLINOIS

Enterprise Rail Park in Effingham in 1999—lots of empty space, and fertile ground for possibilities. (Photograph courtesy of PJ Ryan)

Enterprise Rail Park in Effingham in 2003—the Effingham Railroad has had a significant impact on industry in the park, which includes Krispy Kreme Doughnut Corporation's Mix and Distribution Plant. (Photograph courtesy of PJ Ryan)

CAPE GIRARDEAU, MISSOURI

Academic Hall, Southeast Missouri State University. The university is one of the city's many calling cards. (Photograph courtesy of Southeast Missouri State University)

The Seabaugh Building, Southeast Missouri State University. Completed in 2001, the $7.9 million facility houses the Polytechnic Institute, which includes the University's Department of Industrial Technology, accredited by the National Association of Industrial Technology. (Photograph courtesy of Southeast Missouri State University)

CAPE GIRARDEAU, MISSOURI

Downtown Cape Girardeau—the preservation of historical buildings is part of the town's vision. (Photograph courtesy of the Cape Girardeau Chamber of Commerce)

The Show Me Center—testimony to a rare partnership between a town and a university. (Photograph courtesy of the Show Me Center)

LEBANON, NEW HAMPSHIRE

The Dartmouth-Hitchcock Medical Center, located in Lebanon, New Hampshire, is the fourth-oldest medical school in the U.S. (Photograph courtesy of Chapin Photography)

The medical community in Lebanon has more than 6,000 employees in a town of only 13,000. (Photograph courtesy of Chapin Photography)

COLUMBUS, INDIANA

Modern sophistication is displayed through the architecture of Columbus City Hall. (Photograph courtesy of Balthazar Korab LTD)

The renowned architecture of Columbus, Indiana is reflected at the Indiana Bell Switching Center. (Photograph courtesy of Balthazar Korab LTD)

TUPELO, MISSISSIPPI

The Tupelo Furniture Market encompasses 1.5 million square feet of exhibition space for area furniture manufacturers to showcase products. (Photograph courtesy of the Community Development Foundation of Tupelo/Lee County Mississippi)

The Advanced Education Center, a $15 million workforce training facility, is cohabitated by the University of Mississippi, Itawamba Community College, and Mississippi University for Women, with over one million dollars from local Community Development Foundation industries. (Photograph courtesy of the Community Development Foundation of Tupelo/Lee County Mississippi)

Key #5: Encourage an Entrepreneurial Spirit

L ook deeply into any prospering small town, and you'll find an entrepreneurial spirit manifesting itself in any number of ways. In fact, a town can't have too many entrepreneurs because they can help it thrive. Just look at Philadelphia, Mississippi, one of the Top 100 Agurbs in America (See Appendix A), thanks in part to the Yates Company. This regional construction company employs 4,100 people and was ranked #272 on the list of largest private companies compiled by *Forbes* magazine in 2003.

Although entrepreneurs often tend primarily to their own self-interests, it's an enlightened self-interest—one that takes into account the bigger picture of town prosperity—that drives many towns to success. Nurture these people, and give them room to operate. Towns that recognize that the better their entrepreneurs do, the better the town will do, generally find themselves on a positive growth curve.

Take Santa Claus, Indiana, for example, a community that took its distinctive name from a town meeting on Christmas Eve in the mid-1800s. In 1946, Louis Koch built an amusement park in the tiny burg and named it Santa Claus Land (renamed Holiday World in 1984). When Louis' son Bill returned from World War II, he moved to Santa Claus and eventually bought the park from his siblings. Slowly, Bill Koch added to the park. Within 20 years, the population of Santa Claus had steadily climbed and the town was incorporated.

That's when Bill turned his attention to not just building the theme park into an attraction but also building his town into a model community. He built the first subdivision in the town, appropriately named Christmas Lake Village, bought and moved the first bank into town, started the town's shopping center and built its golf course. He recruited the first manufacturing plant, Kimball, and donated the land on which the company built. In other words, Bill was a one-man economic development dynamo.

Although Bill died in 2001, his wife and children continue to operate Holiday World in the manner that he established, including such unique offerings as free, unlimited soft drinks for everyone at the park. His son Will, who formerly worked for a large defense contractor, is now president of Holiday World. Will says, "In my experience at a larger company I realized that I just got to see one little piece of the whole picture. And I never really got to know who the customer was or what the marketing was about. Here I'm solving problems all of the time and thinking strategically about the business." Today, Holiday World hires more than 1,000 people during the summer season and brings in almost one million visitors per year. The town itself has grown from a few people in Will Koch's grandfather's time to more than 2,000 residents today.

The Entrepreneurial Spirit

Entrepreneurs like the Koch family have a vision for themselves and their businesses and a plan for making their ventures succeed. Often that plan circumvents the more traditional routes of doing business, although good entrepreneurs indeed know what is necessary to take care of their own business and pour all their energy into those efforts.

Two characteristics set successful entrepreneurs apart from other citizens: their ability to see opportunities that others don't and their acumen in knowing when to take calculated risks to achieve their goals. Apart from being an expert in his or her chosen field, a successful entrepreneur must be able to master five areas. So must a town:

Leave your comfort zone. It's safe to say that Louis Koch's idea of building a theme park in Santa Claus, Indiana, was met with some resistance and skepticism, if not outright shock. And the expansion ideas that his son Bill put forth probably caused some discomfort and squirming among town residents as well. Today, Santa Claus is a big tourist attraction. But where would the town be if it had not followed the Koch family's lead and left its comfort zone in the latter part of the 20th century? Probably not on the map. If it still existed, it would be a forlorn and forgotten community with a depressed economy, a place that all tourists would avoid and that its own young people would flee from.

Expanded Horizons

Dick Cabela ran a furniture business in Chappell, Nebraska (population: 983), when he attended a trade show in Chicago in 1961. The show didn't help him grow his furniture business, but he came home with an idea that helped him expand his horizons. Armed with fishing flies and a few ideas about how to start his new business, Cabela began a mail-order business by initially offering "12 hand-tied flies for $1."

With each order for hand-tied flies, Dick and his wife Mary included a catalog of other outdoor items, such as fishing poles, sleeping bags, guns and clothes. Their fledgling mail-order business slowly began to grow. By 1969 the couple moved Cabela's, Inc., to nearby Sidney, Nebraska, where they have been ever since.

The growth hasn't stopped. To its booming catalog business, Cabela's has added retail mega-stores along major interstates in the upper Midwest. (Their second retail store was established in Kearney, Nebraska, one of the top 100 agurbs; see Appendix A.) They mail more than 60 million catalogs each year to all 50 states and to 120 countries. Dick Cabela, in true entrepreneurial fashion, says, "To say that Cabela's has come a long way is a huge understatement; to say that Cabela's has reached its full potential is a huge miscalculation."

Towns trying to expand their comfort zones must face two enemies: *status quo* and *fear of failure.* Together, they make a powerful tag-team intent on deterring expansion into new areas of growth. Those who pay heed to status quo and fear of failure find the pull and sway of these two enemies irresistible; it's like trying to run in a vat of waist-deep, thick, rich molasses. You're not going to get anywhere very quickly.

Unfortunately, you'll see this attitude in too many small towns. It's particularly noticeable in former oil, mining and steel towns or other towns that have experienced an economic setback. Rather than picking themselves up and refocusing their strengths, they simply give up. Overcoming status quo and fear of failure requires winning people over with the PEOPLE approach (See Chapter 3).

Towns can facilitate entrepreneurial growth in a number of ways: through the zoning and permitting processes, through incubators for business start-up, through mentoring and through service organizations that assist business start-up and growth. Even then, a town can squelch entrepreneurship. One

Illinois town received a multi-million dollar federal project in the late 1980s that should have revitalized it. Instead, the civic leaders squabbled and routinely erected obstacles whenever local citizens offered ideas on how to capitalize on the project. Because the civic leaders were not able to move outside their comfort zone, the town lost a golden opportunity to prosper and grow.

You don't have to continually look to leave your comfort zone. If your town is prospering, if things are clicking and running smoothly, if you feel your community is nearing its potential in the key areas that affect its success, then there's no reason to expand that zone. Just maintain what you have and keep pushing forward as planned. But when those plans aren't adequate for taking your community to the next level or for helping it pull out of an economic slump or brain drain, consider looking beyond what you currently do to nurture entrepreneurship.

Take calculated risks. Life is not a risk-free venture. No matter how good a driver you are, you take a risk whenever you get behind the wheel. No matter how good an employee you are, you take a risk working for your company

Industry's Fair Share

It is possible for a community to encourage an entrepreneurial approach without having the backing of the entire town. Some towns, for example, attract out-of-town entrepreneurs—particularly in manufacturing and high-tech industries—by establishing Tax Increment Financing (TIF) or Enterprise Zones (E/Z).

Some local citizens perceive these financial incentives as unfair; they don't see the long-term benefits that accrue to the town with increased economic activity, new jobs and other improvements. Yet in 2002, when the American Farmland Trust looked at the cost of community services during the preceding 15 years in nearly 100 towns, townships and counties, it found that, for the median cost per dollar of tax paid locally, industry uses $0.27 in services. In contrast, residents use $1.16 in services. In my hometown of Effingham, Illinois, a new industry is offered a 10-year tax abatement on property taxes. If you assume a new $5 million plant, the normal annual property tax would be $112,000. Using a three-percent inflation factor for both cost of services and taxes, the community is out of pocket for the first 10 years of abatement but gains it all back by the 14th year—and those gains total a net amount of $8 million over a 50-year period. When you consider the new jobs created in the community, you would probably see a net gain in the first several years.

or within your chosen field. No matter how good a person you might be, bad things can happen. Neither attaining nor maintaining success is guaranteed, whether you're talking about individuals, businesses or towns. People stumble, dynasties crumble, big businesses go belly up.

Yet while many things are out of your control, you can control how you respond to them. When you are willing to take calculated risks, your chances for success—and for rebounding from failure—improve dramatically. People—and towns—with a penchant for taking risks are often admired by others who don't have the same gumption and foresight.

A Sweet Business

The Heath family of Robinson, Illinois, opened the doors of its Heath Brothers Confectionary in 1914 and by 1928 had come up with the ingredients for "English Toffee." Although they sold the confectionary during the Depression, the Heath brothers kept their candy-making equipment and continued to produce Heath English Toffee.

"One day in the late spring of 1942, a man from Washington walked into the Heath company office and asked to see a Mr. Heath," recalls Dick Heath in *Bittersweet: The Story of the Heath Candy Co.* (Tales Press, 1994). "The Army had done some tests on candy to determine what would be best suited for supplying the troops. These tests had found that besides being good candy, because of the pure ingredients, the Heath bar had a relatively long shelf life. Based on the tests and needs, the Army placed its first order for $175,000 worth of Heath bars. That was a lot of nickel candy bars." It was, in fact, more than the company was selling annually at that time, but its owners calculated that they could meet the demand.

The GIs returned with a taste for the Heath Toffee Bar, and the company's sales skyrocketed. The Heath family shared its success with Robinson which, in 1969 and 1970, became the smallest town to ever host a Professional Golf Association Tour event. In 1989 the Heath family sold the company to Leaf, Inc., of Finland, which expanded the plant in Robinson and hired 300 additional employees. In 1997, the Robinson plant became a subsidiary of the Hershey candy company. The impact of the Heaths, however, remains a strong one for Robinson residents.

What many people and towns don't realize is that staying with the status quo brings its own risks. Although comforting, the status quo can lead to isolation and decay. When certain industries are failing or drying up, and your town sticks by those industries as its main source of employment and income, you're inviting trouble. At that point, the bigger risk is remaining with the status quo. On the other hand, the consequences of taking well-thought-out risks can mean the difference between merely surviving and really thriving.

Knowing when to take a risk is as important as drumming up the courage to do so. One time to consider taking risks is when the future isn't so bright and you see storm clouds on the horizon. Your motivation is to avoid the storm and sidestep the danger. The second time to take risks is when the horizon is clear but you see opportunities for greater things. For instance, your current business may be profitable and operating smoothly, but you see a chance for expansion and greater profits. At the community level, your economy is strong but you see the opportunity to stabilize the economic base even more by adding companies in industries that would be new to the community but are forecast to do well.

Towns tend to fall into one of three risk-taking categories. Some never take risks, regardless of the situation (and typically suffer in the long run). Some take risks only when forced to do so—when they realize that not doing so would clearly lead to their demise. And other towns take calculated risks even when all is well, because they have an eye to the future and an entrepreneurial bent. The latter group takes destiny into its own hands and, more often than not, comes out on top.

The decision to take a risk can be made easier by weighing the pros and cons. Stack up the expected or hoped-for outcomes and benefits of making a move against the associated costs and risks. For example, if the main source of income in your community is the textile industry and the main two companies in your town are either laying off many people or contemplating relocations, consider other ways to resuscitate your economy and your town. Look to your strengths—your workforce, location and other industries—and consider what is most likely to revive the economy. Always rely heavily on your strengths in taking on a new venture. Taking risks boils down to finding ways to take greater advantage of your community's strengths.

As you venture into new territory, maintain balance and control. In other words, don't put all your eggs into one basket. You don't want to lose everything if the venture fails, so take trial runs, if possible. Advance cautiously, and allow leeway for reshaping plans as situations unfold. Taking risks doesn't mean going blindly into something, or going at it with abandon; you calculate your risks not only before you take them but also as you take them.

Learn from failure. W.E. Hickson penned the famous words,

"'Tis a lesson you should heed,

Try, try again.

If at first you don't succeed,

Try, try again."

Thomas Edison, the American inventor, took Hickson's words to heart. In 1879, after spending $40,000 (equivalent to $700,000 today) and performing 1,200 experiments, he succeeded in producing electric light by using carbonized filaments from cotton thread.

One thousand, two hundred experiments! Can you imagine failing at something more than 1,000 times, shaking your head, grinning determinedly and trying another couple hundred times? Edison obviously had no fear of failure. His eventual success was a tribute not just to his genius but also to his persistence and his ability to learn from his previous attempts to create electric light.

Durango, Colorado: A Different Way of Thinking

Originally a railroad and mining town started in the 1880s, Durango, Colorado, experienced rapid growth in the latter part of the 20th century. It takes advantage of its location near the southern edge of the San Juan Mountains to offer skiing and operates the historic Durango & Silverton Narrow Gauge Railroad. The town holds an array of events and festivals throughout the year, drawing visitors and tourists to its Main Avenue Historic District.

"We are in a constant struggle to define ourselves. Some call us a resort town, but we're actually a real working town," says Bobby Lieb, director of the Durango Chamber of Commerce. "While we are a very pretty town that people like to visit, we still have a manufacturing base, business parks, agriculture and even oil and gas. In fact, we are the largest natural gas producer in the state of Colorado."

Tourism provides Durango with 24 percent of its employment base, but natural gas brings in 60 percent of the property tax revenue in the county. Many people are relocating to the town because of its quality of life. Certainly Durango is taking advantage of its natural resources—yet many other towns in similar situations don't take advantage of their own strengths because they're afraid to change.

Failure is not the end. Failure is part of a learning process. It adds to your knowledge and understanding of a system, a field or a pursuit by refining your ideas. The real failure is in not trying again.

Understand the need to change. Think of the advancements made in the past 10 years in computers and other technology. Companies still using technology that is behind the times are limiting their effectiveness and ability to operate.

The same can happen in small towns, where business is often based on a handshake with someone you see every day. Relationships and histories take on a different, more personal tenor in small towns, and this can complicate the decision to change—even when those decisions are logical and made in the best interests of the town. Thus, you see some towns mired in the past, unable to bring in new industry or improve how they do business because they're following in their fathers' and grandfathers' footsteps. They can't break with their past in favor of a more favorable future.

Towns that see change as a necessary component of community health will stay a step ahead, remain prosperous or get on the road to revitalization. Change is the vehicle that keeps you moving forward on that road to success or revival.

Be proactive rather than reactive. Say your town often floods because it's by a river. Hearing that torrential rains are moving into your area, you sandbag outside your house and put up on bricks everything in the basement that could be damaged by water. Meanwhile, your neighbor does nothing. Big rains have been predicted before and never come; he doesn't believe the forecast this time.

When the rains come and the streets flood, a half-inch of water seeps into your basement. But it doesn't touch any of your possessions because of the bricks you put down. Your neighbor, however, has six inches of water in his basement and many ruined items. As he looks in disgust at all of the water, he thinks of the resulting damage and of the clean-up work that now awaits him.

The proactive approach—preparing for the rains—was obviously the wiser choice. Being proactive has many advantages, some practical, some psychological. Being proactive:

- Enables you to do something about a situation rather than waiting for something to happen and awaiting the outcome. This gives you a feeling of control (or at least helps you feel you can affect the outcome).
- Gets you moving by removing the physical tension and mental anxiety of waiting and wondering. You'll experience a freeing, energizing feeling.
- Gives you forward momentum. This movement is often the difference between a successful entrepreneur and someone who wishes to be one.
- Affords you the opportunity to make mistakes. You have time to recover and adjust, an opportunity lost if you are making mistakes in the reactive mode. Quite often, in reaction you find yourself behind the 8-ball, with one shot to take—which means you feel greater pressure to achieve everything all at once.
- Gives you a good feeling about yourself and your actions. People generally feel good about themselves when they're doing something rather than thinking about doing something and wondering if it will work.
- Diminishes the fear of failure and its companion, fear of the unknown. You realize that action—even if it's not perfect—is better than no action at all. Because you know you have time to recover and adjust, your fear of failure will diminish or disappear.
- Gives you a head start. You'll be farther along than those who are reactive.
- Encourages you to attempt and thus achieve more. You're not so guarded and defensive when you're proactive.

Being proactive is all about attitude and outlook. Don't just wildly strike out in new areas, attempting things outside your realm of expertise, or enter into new ventures without careful planning and thinking. Instead, adopt a proactive attitude, one that combines readiness for action with wisdom in preparing for that action. It's not about just moving first; it's about moving when the time is right and in the right manner.

Moving when the time is right takes foresight, wisdom and courage. Many people might have the foresight to see change is needed but have neither the wisdom to know the best course of action nor the courage to take it. When you combine all three elements—foresight, wisdom and courage—you have the ingredients to be proactive and to put yourself and your town ahead of the game.

Key #6: Maintain Local Control

I n a small town, you don't have a lot of red tape to cut through; the channels of government are not usually difficult to maneuver. And, compared to large cities, a greater percent of people in small towns are usually more active in their communities because they know they can make a difference. This community involvement and sense of control contribute to the attractiveness and prosperity of many small towns.

Another aspect of control involves local ownership. In a small town, you'll typically find that townspeople own financial institutions and newspapers, as well as businesses in the retail, manufacturing and service sectors. The town with local ownership in these areas has a much greater chance of being strong and vibrant than the town without.

Just ask the residents of Mattoon, Illinois, home to Consolidated Communications (originally known as the Mattoon Telephone Company). Started in 1894 by Iverson A. Lumpkin, the family-owned company grew into one of the largest non-Bell telephone companies in the United States. Richard A. (Dick) Lumpkin, the founder's great-grandson, returned to Mattoon after earning an MBA at Harvard and transformed the business from a sleepy, rural phone company into one involved in telephone directory publishing, fiber optic networks, cellular, cable TV and other related activities. In 1998 the company merged with McLeodUSA.

Unfortunately, McLeodUSA expanded too rapidly and was brought down in the telecom crash of 2001. Dick Lumpkin teamed with two private equity funds to buy back Consolidated Communications when McLeodUSA was forced to sell the business to pay off bondholders. More than 700 local employees of Consolidated Communications breathed a collective sigh of relief when it was announced in July 2002 that the company was returning to Lumpkin's leadership.

The influence of someone like Dick Lumpkin (and his ancestors) upon a town and entire region is difficult to quantify. He has donated time and money to numerous causes ranging from the Special Olympics to building Eastern Illinois University's Lumpkin School of Business. He also established the economic development group for his home county and has been active in a number of other community programs and developments.

Local people like Lumpkin care more about where they live and thus will be motivated to make decisions based on the long- and short-term welfare of the community. And, while people in small communities still make mistakes, they also have more power to make corrections—without an outsider's approval—if they maintain local control. The town that has local ownership holds its destiny in its hands.

Consider control on an individual basis for a moment. Say you work for a company whose many rules and regulations seem to have been put in place simply to control (and perhaps demean) the workforce. The president of the company—often referred to as "The Dictator"—lives three states away and rarely visits the plant. Workers have little say in how the work environment is set up and maintained. The equipment often breaks down, affecting production quotas. Yet if you raise the topic of equipment failure with management, you are labeled a troublemaker. You quickly learn that you have no control over your work environment and become unmotivated, cynical, depressed or despairing—or a combination of all four.

Now imagine working for another manufacturer. The company president lives in town, the few rules and regulations are for the benefit and safety of the employees, the employees have a voice in how the plant operates and the equipment is well maintained. When something breaks down, management responds quickly and also invites feedback from workers on how to improve the work environment and increase productivity. Certainly production and profit are important, but there is a pervading sense of teamwork among management and laborers and a feeling of genuine concern for the employees. You *do* have a voice at this plant; you *do* have some control over your work world. Your overall outlook will likely be more positive and optimistic in such a setting because you have some control over your environment. You know you can actually do something to improve matters if a problem arises.

Several Important Sectors

Local ownership in two areas—financial institutions and newspapers—can greatly aid a town's development.

Tell City, Indiana, is in the midst of economic recovery, thanks in large part to a $5-million unsecured line of credit set up by locally owned banks to assist the community in building a rail line into town (See Chapter 3). Ironically, many of the banks involved in offering this credit have since been purchased by larger institutions and are no longer locally owned. (In fact, the number of community banks has dwindled from 12,366 in 1980 to 10,180 in 1990 to 6,936 in 2002, according to FDIC's Reports of Condition and Income.) Officials in Tell City doubt that banks owned from afar would have extended such a large line of credit to them.

They have good reason to doubt. A small-town bank owned by a distant conglomerate or mega-bank has little say or power in providing loans for local projects. Small towns are small change to mega-banks more intent on cutting deals with large corporations throughout the nation and world. Officials at these mega-banks may be well-meaning, but common sense dictates that they pay attention to big cities, big corporations and big money.

The Effingham Railroad: Proving the Experts Wrong

No one builds new railroads these days. Still, in the late 1990s, I decided to build a new railroad in my hometown of Effingham, Illinois. Charlie Barenfanger, who had operated a short-line railroad, and I decided that, with the consolidation taking place in the rail industry, we could offer companies a competitive advantage in locating a new plant along our railroad. Because our railroad would connect with CSX and the Illinois Central (IC) and depend upon both railroads for business, we approached their economic development departments.

Neither company was helpful; in fact, the head of economic development for the IC was outright hostile. He said we were crazy to spend the roughly $1 million it would take to build the line and would be lucky if we moved more than 200 cars per year. To this day his words ring in my head: "You know, son, if a new industry was going to move into Effingham, the Illinois Central would bring it in!" When I pointed out that the IC hadn't brought a new industry into town in more than 30 years, he replied, "And it's not likely you will either."

Within four years we had facilitated the creation of several hundred high-paying jobs by attracting projects such as Krispy Kreme's national manufacturing and distribution center. By 2003 we were already handling 10 times the number of cars that the "rail expert" had predicted we'd do in our best year and had developed a profitable side business. If we had listened to the IC employee instead of pushing ahead and doing what we believed made sense for our local community, those hundreds of jobs would still be a pipe dream.

Local bankers, on the other hand, can find the time to talk with local business executives at a downtown café. They have just as much to gain from an investment as the local business folks and the town itself; they're all in it together. A town with locally owned financial institutions that embrace the town's vision for growth and vitality can grow that vision to the size of the banks' backing. Such institutions are, in effect, putting their money where their mouth is.

Often, what stalls a community's growth is not a lack of vision or leadership but a lack of capital. That capital is often more readily accessible through locally owned banks. Certainly, you have to present a solid, detailed plan for how that capital will be used and show why it's a wise investment in the community. And when you do so, you know you have the ear of your local bankers, because they have as much reason to want the community to thrive as you do.

Take ABC Bancorp, for example. Headquartered in Moultrie, Georgia, ABC Bancorp has $1.2 billion in assets and 34 locations in Georgia, Alabama and Florida. "Our economic development group learned that Farmland National Beef was looking for a facility to process meat for Wal-Mart. Our city, state and economic development group all expressed interest in exploring their coming to our town," says Jack Hunnicutt, president of ABC Bancorp. "When the company made a return visit to explore the subject further I was asked to be present. It's funny how everything ends up coming down to money. We needed the jobs, and money and loaning that money are what we are all about. At the meeting I committed us to a multi-million dollar loan to get them to Moultrie. By the end of the day we had a deal signed.

"The advantage of being local is that we could make the decision on the spot," Hunnicutt continues. "With bigger banks, a lot of the time you have to go through a lot of different layers of management and committees." The meat-processing facility now employs 350 people.

Like banks, newspapers also play an important role in town development. They inform readers of the opportunities and risks involved, provide a forum for discussion of town growth and development and serve as an advocate for growth coupled with fiscal responsibility, all with the long-term picture in mind. Papers owned by national conglomerates simply will not have the same emotional or financial investments in the local community that locally owned papers do.

Astoria, Oregon: Banking on Help

Astoria, at the mouth of the Columbia River in northwestern Oregon, knows all about local control. The Forrester family has owned *The Daily Astorian* since 1914; Gimre's Shoes, Home Baking and Knutsen Insurance have all been locally owned for 80 or more years.

The Astoria Mill had a long history in town as well. Built in the 1870s, the mill shut down in 1989 and left behind an industrial eyesore beset with decades of toxic contamination. The U.S. Small Business Administration (SBA), the mill's major creditor, seized and auctioned machinery, roofs and siding; the county seized what it believed to be uncontaminated property for nonpayment of taxes.

"The SBA estimated a clean-up of $1 to $2 million and the property was only worth $800,000. They decided it was so contaminated that they didn't want to touch it," says Paul Benoit, Astoria's community development director during the cleanup. "The site became the town dump—and it was right in the middle of our downtown! The community looks at the riverfront as their own. There is no 'someone else's backyard' in a small, rural town. It's everyone's front yard."

City officials wanted to not only clean up the mill site but also redeem it by attracting a developer. "We had a vision that was broadly supported by the community," Benoit remembers. "It was this idea of a community that was lifting itself up. Rather than just singing the blues, we were doing something about it—something innovative."

Stephen Forrester, publisher of *The Daily Astorian*, agrees. "We (the newspaper) took hold of this clean-up project. We saw the importance of it for the long-term benefit to the community. Building the community is what we are about." *The Daily Astorian* featured many stories on the progress of the Astoria Mill project to keep the community informed along the way.

Astoria worked with the Oregon Department of Environmental Quality (ODEQ), which agreed to environmentally clean the property if the city came up with 50 percent of the clean-up cost. That meant the city of fewer than 10,000 had to come up with about $700,000.

Benoit found that the banks with outside owners had no interest in helping Astoria. But two locally owned institutions—Shorebank Enterprises and Bank of Astoria—agreed to help in less than one week. Once the clean-up was completed, the property was sold to a group developing a mixed-use project that will eventually include 200 living units and a credit union headquarters.

Today there are fewer locally owned papers than at any other time in the last century. According to the Death Tax Newsletter, produced by the *Seattle Times* for family-owned newspapers, the United States had 2,100 independently owned newspapers in 1910. Seventy years later, that number had plummeted to 700; by 2003 it stood at fewer than 300. Although small in numbers, independently owned newspapers have a singular voice that speaks for their communities in ways that publishing conglomerates can't.

Take, for example, the role of Alabama's *Decatur Daily* and its editor and publisher from 1924 through 1984, Barrett C. Shelton, Sr. Shelton had a vision to revive northern Alabama's economy in the late 1940s, and he coordinated the long effort that made that vision a reality.

In the 1940s northern Alabama was one of the poorest sections of not only the state but also the entire country. Virtually all the industrial promotion taking place in the state was done by Alabama Power; because the company didn't serve northern Alabama, it had little incentive to promote the region. In 1949 the state as a whole had twice the number of manufacturing jobs per county that northern Alabama had.

Tom Johnson, who had established Alabama Power's New Industries Division, was approached by Barrett Shelton and the manager of the local utility supply company, Quince Eddens, about heading up a northern Alabama economic development group. Johnson agreed, provided he had a $30,000 annual budget. Said Eddens, "Barrett and I got with the utility board and suggested they put up $15,000 and we'll go over to Huntsville and invite their utility board to put up the other $15,000. Well, by Jove! Huntsville said they would go along with us, so we hired Tom, made his salary satisfactory to him, and let him use the rest of the money as he saw fit."

Through his newspaper, Shelton tirelessly promoted the idea of the regional initiative, as opposed to each small community fighting against one another for jobs. Other towns eventually joined Huntsville and Decatur, enabling the group to raise its annual budget to $500,000 today. Companies have flocked to northern Alabama due to these efforts. The 12 counties that make up the Northern Alabama Industrial Development Association now have 70 percent more jobs per county than the rest of the state. In one 10-year period alone, 73,899 new jobs were created with a total investment of $8 billion. (Agurbs within this region include Russellville in Franklin County, Double Springs in Winston County, Scottsboro in Jackson County and Ft. Payne in DeKalb County.)

Newspapers such as *Decatur Daily* are more likely to lead the charge, at least publicly, when they have local connections. The main interests of a paper owned by a national conglomerate are selling more newspapers and selling more advertising. Local publishers and editors, on the other hand, tend to see more of the community "soul," take more of a long-term view and generally try to take a more positive approach for the community.

Local ownership is also important in the retailing, manufacturing and service sectors of town. These sectors provide much of the energy for business growth and advancement and are key players in shaping the vision for the town. As with banks and newspapers, locally owned outfits will be more invested in community growth and concerned about the town's long-term welfare.

Paris, Illinois: a *Beacon* of Light

The Paris Beacon Publishing Company of Illinois publishes the *Paris Beacon-News*, a newspaper that began as a weekly in 1848 and became a daily in 1898. Owned and managed by the Jenison family since 1926, the paper has received numerous awards, including the 2002 Mississippi Valley Family Business of the Year Award for excellence in industry and positive impact on its community.

The Jenison family has been active in a number of community projects over the years. Ed Jenison, who worked for the paper for 54 years until his death in 1996, spent three terms as a U.S. congressman. His son Ned joined the company in 1959, and the next generation—represented by Ned's son, Kevin—came on board in 1978. Today, four Jenisons serve as officers of the company, and six own the corporate stock.

Dave Sullivan, president of the local First Bank and Trust, says of Ned's role in the community, "Ned has been on the board of our local economic development group for a long time. I can't think of the number of times that Ned has written positive articles and editorials about our economic development activities and the involvement of local governmental bodies."

Kevin Jenison says, "We don't really view ourselves as leaders in Paris, but we do try to make it a better place in which to live. In many respects we are the only real voice for our citizens or for our government to help get the news out about the town. We've been involved in several projects that helped make this a better place to live." For instance, the family has helped improve the city parks and is now working on a new treatment plant to improve the quality of local water.

That doesn't mean it's bad to have chain stores in town; they can provide a steady source of jobs and a boost to the economy. In fact, such stores can attract business from surrounding towns and make your town the place to go for hardware items or for discount retail purchases. In many small towns, national chains provide the main source of employment. The leadership and input a town receives from locally owned manufacturers and retailers, however, will be *greater* than from the national chains. The national chains have goals and visions of their own, which don't necessarily compete against the town's goals—but aren't necessarily in step with them, either.

Key #7: Build Your Brand

A lmost everything has a brand, whether good or bad, strong or ineffectual. Brands are often encapsulated with a slogan: *Just do it. It's The Real Thing. The breakfast of champions.* You probably identified the products associated with those slogans as Nike, Coca-Cola and Wheaties. These products are well-branded; their images have come to mean something distinct to most people. That's what a brand is: A vehicle to distinguish a product, a company or a person from the crowd. It's a personal message about the product, company or person. It promises something; you expect the same thing from that product, company or person every time. Think about when you go grocery shopping. Chances are you buy the same brand of barbecue sauce, the same brand of ketchup, the same brand of cereal every time—because you've grown accustomed to them and like the taste and the value. When you shop for blue jeans, shirts, suits or shoes, do you usually look for the same brands again and again because of the quality and comfort? When you want to buy a car, do you make distinctions between different car makers (or, for that matter, between different car *sellers*)?

An effective brand helps you make those distinctions and know what to expect. There's no guessing with an effective and accurate brand. A McDonald's cheeseburger will taste the same whether you buy it in southern California, northern Maine or western Illinois. Every Mercedes-Benz will be smooth-riding, elegant and top quality. Rockport shoes promise to be durable, sturdy and comfortable.

What branding does for companies, products and people, it also does for towns. It sets them apart by giving the region, state or even the nation notice of what it's about and what it offers. A brand is a town's calling card—it can put a town on a map and keep it there for all the world to see.

If you're located in the middle of nowhere, without a strong population base for hundreds of miles, you had better develop something that sets you apart from everyone else. That is just what the people of Mackinac Island did in 1898, when they decided not to allow any motorized vehicles on their island in upper Michigan. Back then, the island's residents probably didn't think about establishing a brand for their community—but that's exactly what they did. Today Mackinac Island bills itself as the "All Natural" theme park of America. The island is 80 percent state park and 20 percent Victorian village. The island's natural beauty, its relaxed pace and its lack of motorized traffic (though there are plenty of horse-drawn carriages), make for a seductive draw. In fact, more than one million people annually visit the island, which has about 500 permanent residents.

Delivering Your Town's Message

Big cities have brands. Think for a moment of New York. Chicago. Washington, D.C. Los Angeles. Las Vegas. San Francisco. Minneapolis. Each city conjures up a different image that reflects distinct strengths, cultures and passions.

It's no different with small towns. Branson, Missouri, has its own brand. So does Leavenworth, Washington. And so do Mackinac Island, Michigan, with its Victorian charm and lack of motorized vehicles, and Tombstone, Arizona, which stages daily reenactments of the Shootout at the O.K. Corral. But these towns didn't work at achieving their brand; they worked at achieving their vision.

If that's the case, why all the fuss about brands? If you don't have to work at them, then why should you pay any attention to them? True, you shouldn't focus your initial efforts on your brand. But as your town's brand takes shape, cultivate that brand, use it to its fullest extent, refine it and make sure that outsiders are catching your message. It might surprise you that your town has a message, but it does—whether it has been consciously crafted or not. That message is delivered to outsiders each time they visit your town and to your townspeople on a daily basis.

A few years ago, a national restaurant chain was ready to build a restaurant in a west-central Illinois town, but at the last moment the restaurant executives changed their minds. Why? Because the road leading from the municipal airport to the downtown area went through a rundown residential section and a rather bleak industrial area. These images didn't represent a true picture of the town, but they branded the community in the executives' minds as a poor, ill-kept town that wouldn't be able to support a restaurant. The executives said, "No thanks," and retraced their route through the same rundown neighborhoods and industrial areas, never to set foot in the town again.

Was this a fair assessment of the town? No. It was the first impression—and, unfortunately, a wrong and inaccurate impression. Even though it was based on incomplete evidence, this glance at the town gave the restaurant executives all they needed to know to deem the community as one in which their business would not prosper.

Contrast that to the experience of the *Wall Street Journal,* which fell in love with Highland, Illinois, the first time company executives drove into the town. The executives were given a tour of Highland by the town's economic development director, who showed off the town's best features. The result? The *Journal* chose Highland as the location for a new printing plant for its Midwest edition.

What are the first impressions of people who come into your town as visitors? What do they see when they enter town? Are there signs of vibrancy and health—or of decay and neglect? Are the residential areas that are most evident to outsiders kept clean and well-tended? What type of image comes from the business district, the industrial parks and the main thoroughfare through your town?

Think of driving through other small communities. You get a certain sense of each community as you drive through, don't you? The town's storefronts and streets, its parks and houses, the landscaping and the land itself, all murmur a subtle message about the type of town it is. This message is magnified by personal encounters with residents in restaurants, stores, the chamber of commerce office or wherever you meet its people. Some towns are open and welcoming to visitors, while others tolerate outsiders but do little to extend their stay or to compel them to move to the town. Other towns might be open to visitors and want them to come, but they don't present an image that matches their desires. Such was the case with the Illinois town that lost the restaurant bid.

To effectively deliver your town's message, you don't need to form a branding committee that works long into the night to come up with a catchy slogan or a slick marketing campaign. You do need to help people see your town's strengths and capabilities and what it offers or promises. In fact, the best way to build a town brand and to effectively deliver it is to have a vision for your town, shape goals from that vision and achieve those goals. In other words, do what you do best.

If you consistently achieve your goals, you create your brand along the way. You become known for what you produce or for what type of town you are. Your strengths and advantages become evident to those who enter your town, hear about it or read about it. Branding is not a tool that is produced separately from everything else your town does; it evolves from the process of achieving your goals, being consistent and knowing and using your strengths to your advantage.

Coming Through on Promises

A brand's value is not based on the quality of the product. Quality, of course, is important to the product's success. But the real value lies in a brand's ability to deliver what it says it will deliver when it says it will deliver it.

What would you think if you bought a box of Tide laundry detergent and it didn't get the dirt out of your clothes? Or if you bought a can of Maxwell House coffee and it wasn't "good to the last drop?" Or suppose you bought a Chevy S-10 Pickup and it wasn't built "like a rock" but rather like a lemon? You'd probably switch to a different detergent, change your brand of coffee and look at other trucks in the future. There is an old saying: "Do something good and people will tell one person. Do something bad and they will tell 20 people."

The same holds true for a town. If someone visiting a tourist town receives poor service and meets inhospitable people, chances are that tourist won't return—or speak well of the town to his or her friends and neighbors. (And if the tourist is a travel writer, the town is in real trouble!) If a college town provides inadequate accommodations and services for an academic convention, that event probably won't return. If manufacturers in a manufacturing town are consistently late in delivering orders, customers will be wary about doing future business with them. In these cases, the town's brand is damaged because it's not delivering what it has promised to deliver or is expected to deliver. When a town doesn't come through on its promises, it damages its reputation and weakens its perceived value.

If a town comes through as promised and delivers as advertised, it solidifies its reputation and is true to its brand. It confirms in people's minds what they held to be true: This is a great college town, a great tourist town or a great retirement town. When a town consistently delivers what is expected, it will become known in wider circles and be in a position to grow its brand.

Different Towns, Different Directions

Danville and Decatur are two Illinois towns that have battled sullied reputations in recent years. Both are blue-collar, manufacturing, "Rust Belt" towns that struggled, both economically and image-wise, throughout the late 1980s and early 1990s.

Danville hired a dynamic local economic developer, projected a progressive image and developed a "Bricks to Chips" image campaign. Bricks were part of the town's old history, while chips—as in computer technology—represented the new vision. That vision is being played out in the strides Danville has made in recent years to be a mover in the high-tech world:

- Alcoa has built a $300 million plant in Danville, creating 200 new jobs to manufacture rolled aluminum for the aerospace and automotive industries.

- Systrand Presta Engines Systems has created 50 new jobs in Danville through a $20 million investment that includes an 80,000 square-foot plant. The company, which produces ready-to-install camshafts, is a joint venture of German and U. S. companies.

- Owens-Corning and IKO Industries partnered to produce Fiberteq, LLC, which produces fiberglass mat for the roofing industry. The $50 million joint venture resulted in 70 new jobs for Danville-area residents.

Contrast Danville's image to that of Decatur, which received national recognition because of a series of strikes at its top three manufacturers in the early 1990s. A revolving door in the economic development department, infighting on the city council, and an inability to project a positive image have made economic development an uphill battle for Decatur. Too, many executives still associate Decatur with serious labor problems, despite its talented, skilled workforce. As a result, few new industries are willing to move to the troubled town.

Growing Your Brand

"Growing your brand" means extending your reach to become known to more people and businesses. There is a distinction between growing your brand and diversifying your economic base. At first, the two concepts appear at odds with one another.

When you diversify your economic base, you not only become a community of diverse talents, interests and backgrounds but also guard against the downfall of the community if one industry begins to sputter and fail. If that industry were the only one in town, you'd be in deep trouble. By diversifying your base, your economy can remain healthy even if one industry experiences problems. A diverse economy is a healthy economy.

When growing your brand, however, it's best to focus on your core strengths and passions—to grow *deeper*, not *wider*. To grow wider is to diversify which, in branding, confuses the customer, client and consumer. To grow deeper is to solidify, which assures the customer, client and consumer that you are an expert in your brand, that your brand speaks of high quality products or services, and that you are the one to come to for those products or services.

A town is wise to diversify its economic base and to focus its branding on its strengths and vision. A town can't be everything to everybody. When people think of Sierra Vista, Arizona, for example, they think of the amenities that make it a great place to retire. Bisbee, a neighboring community, has evolved into an artist colony; its drawing card is a well-maintained turn-of-the-20th-century downtown that was completely rebuilt after a 1908 fire. That doesn't mean Bisbee is a place solely for artisans or that it doesn't have industries unrelated to artists. The city started as a mining town and still operates a mine, providing jobs for many local citizens.

Likewise, Iowa City, Iowa, home to the University of Iowa, is known mainly as a college town. While its "bread and butter" comes from the university and its brand is distinctly academic, Iowa City also has a variety of industries and businesses that are entirely unrelated to the university.

Growing your brand doesn't mean you don't try to grow your economy. A broad economic base is both healthy and desired, and it doesn't run counter to the deepening effect of growing your brand. The two efforts complement one another. The town that can grow its economic base horizontally while growing its brand vertically will prosper the most.

Branding for the Long Haul

Just as you don't want to confuse outsiders by spreading your brand too thin—by trying to be too many things to too many people—you don't want to confuse them by claiming to be one type of town one year and another the next. If your strength is in manufacturing, or in your medical facilities, or in your technical companies, let it be known. If your strength is in natural resources,

Western North Carolina: Reassessing Its Values

In the early 1990s, Western North Carolina struggled to come up with a fresh approach for recruiting new industry. After looking at the region's strengths, various community leaders recognized there was an "invisible industry" of craftspeople already working in shops, studios, and galleries, many of them located on the back roads of the Blue Ridge Mountains.

The resulting "HandMade in America" initiative publicizes the unique craftsmanship of the region, which contributes more than $120 million annually to the local economy (four times the revenue generated by the "old" industry of burley tobacco). Several road trails have been established that lead visitors to more than 500 sites, including 200 craft studios. (Highlands, Murphy, Sylva, Columbus, Brevard and Boone, North Carolina, are all agurbs in the middle of this regional initiative.)

amenities that appeal to retired folks or academic institutions, spread that message. Celebrate your diversity within, and reinforce your brand without.

Build your brand based on your vision, and build it for the long haul. Take your cue from successful corporations such as McDonald's, Disney and Kodak, which have built strong brands that clearly reflect their value to consumers. Successful corporations are often quite diversified in their business and products, yet they have a brand that communicates distinctly and unmistakably what they are about and what their value is. Successful towns do likewise.

Brands don't appear overnight. They develop slowly, often emerging from a clutter of ideas as the preeminent message. Similarly, brands should be built to last so they can become something on which people can rely—a precious commodity in a world where things change with great speed. Overnight successes and singular ideas, no matter how good or worthy, are like comets streaking across the sky; a brand is like a star, constant and enduring.

Can you change brands? Yes, but it's best to do so only when warranted, such as the case of Leavenworth, Washington, which was forced to abandon its brand as a lumber town. It was most appropriate for Leavenworth to change brands because lumber companies no longer served the community and therefore no longer defined it. In most cases, however, a change is neither warranted nor wise. A tourist town that has experienced a slump should not chuck its brand and try to become something it's not; it should focus on rebounding from the slump. It's disconcerting, even disturbing, to outsiders when they see a town trying to become something it hasn't been before.

Site Seeing

One practical way to grow your community's brand is through a Web site. A Web site can provide an accurate picture (both literally and figuratively) of your town's strengths, vision, resources, opportunities and attitude. Create a site that is visually pleasing, logically organized and clear in its message. Be sure to accentuate the positive and subtly reinforce the idea of your brand.

Don't be afraid to let a little of the town's personality show through. Give the viewers a feel for what your town is like and consider using a slogan to communicate your brand message. "Whitewater, Wisconsin: Relaxing in Wisconsin's Back Yard" and "Hardy County, West Virginia: A Land for the Adventurous" are just two examples.

For a few examples of Web sites developed by small towns and counties, visit the following.

- Hammond, Louisiana (www.hammond.org)
- St. George, Utah (www.sgcity.org)
- Prescott, Arizona's, Chamber of Commerce (www.prescott.,org)
- Nevada County, California (www.mynevadacounty.com)
- Blaine County, Idaho (www.co.blaine.id.us)

Certainly, towns can change just as people can change, and change per se is not bad. In the case of branding, however, undertake change with caution—and only when the brand does not describe what your town is really about or when it doesn't point to where you are headed in the near future.

Focusing on Service and Quality

Every town has something to offer to outsiders, whether it is what local manufacturers produce, the service provided by local medical facilities, the visual attractions of nearby beaches or mountains, or the talent resident in the local college or high-tech community. The clearer your brand is, in terms of what it promises to outsiders, the more it will draw business and the greater your town will profit.

Service and quality are hallmarks of any good business. Towns whose brands are grounded in service and quality will thrive. A tourist town that has high quality in terms of its natural resources and surroundings, but delivers poor service in terms of its motels, bed-and-breakfasts, restaurants and shops, will not measure up to the neighboring town that provides service on a par with its quality. A town whose manufacturers provide good customer service, but have production quality inferior to their competitors, likewise will suffer.

Several towns educate the employees who are most likely to be first contacts for visitors in town—restaurant workers, desk clerks, convenience store clerks and so on—on how quality and service contribute to the town's reputation. There is nothing worse than stopping in a new town and asking someone, "What's there to do in town? Where is a good place to eat?" and hearing this answer: "There's nothing to do here! There's no good place to eat around here!"

When you focus on what your town can do or provide for others, what qualities make it attractive, and what strengths can be used to fill a niche for others, you are well on the way to creating or solidifying your brand.

Key #7½: Embrace the Teeter-Totter Factor

Like many small towns in the Southeast, Mooresville, North Carolina, depended on the textile industry for the bulk of its jobs. When those jobs started to move overseas in the late 1990s, Mooresville reinvented itself. Its claim to fame: It is home to NASCAR's Garage, where most of the nation's stock car teams come between races to tune up and test new technologies and techniques.

The Auto Research Center, built in 2000, offers the most progressive aerodynamic research facility of its kind—a unique wind tunnel for scale-model stock cars. More than 60 race-related shops operate in Mooresville, where more than half of the town works in a NASCAR-related job. NASCAR built its Technical Institute in the town in 2002.

In less than a decade Mooresville lost every one of its many textile plants yet managed to double in population, to more than 18,000 residents. The town offers an example of the final characteristic exhibited by successful small towns: the Teeter-Totter Factor. It's an almost intangible factor and perhaps the hardest of the 7½ keys to consciously work toward and attain.

The Teeter-Totter Factor can be described this way: It takes only a small shift one way or the other to make a negative or positive impact on a community. In other words, a little shift can turn a negative into a positive. And that's good news for communities seeking to change.

The opposite, however, is equally true: A small shift can easily turn a positive into a negative. Thus, there's a precarious balance in small towns. The towns that are aware of this unsteadiness are more likely to keep their weight on the positive end and maintain what they have going for them. Towns that remain unaware of this shifting ability may find themselves, quite suddenly, up in the air.

Up in the Air

Parasailers love being up in the air. Travelers appreciate the convenience of flying in airplanes. And thrill-seekers enjoy the wind in their faces while on a roller coaster or hang glider. But, for the most part, being up in the air is not enjoyable.

The good news for small towns is that you *can* effect change. But if the winds shift, they could take the community in a completely different (and negative) direction. For example, contrast Mooresville, North Carolina, with a town 90 miles to the southeast. Rockingham, North Carolina, has been home to the North Carolina Speedway since 1965. It was also the home of TNS Mills, Inc., which closed in the early 2000s. The numbers in Table 10.1 tell the story of how Rockingham has dwindled while Mooresville has blossomed.

Table 10.1: Rockingham and Mooresville Comparison

	1990		2000	
	Population	Employed	Population	Employed
Rockingham	9,399	4,208	9,672	3,770
Mooresville	9,317	4,528	18,823	9,171

Generally, the Rockinghams of the 21st century will be the ones that campaign for a new state or federal prison—which may not gain them anything for the long term. In fact, Rockingham had a correctional facility for more than 60 years; the facility closed in 1996. Such campaigns, if successful, usually provide a quick fix in terms of construction jobs and then continual employment for guards and services to the prisoners. Yet these jobs offer little upward mobility. In contrast, manufacturing and many service industries translate gains in productivity into higher wages and benefits.

Nashua, Iowa, is another small town that has not capitalized on the potential to reinvent itself. This town of 1,600 has an unemployment rate twice the state average of 3.5 percent, along with a deteriorating economy, rows of empty houses, closed factories and shuttered retail businesses. Set in the woods along the scenic Cedar River, Nashua is a picturesque small town that has noticeably declined, without a plan of how to come out of its funk.

What could it do? Sitting on the outskirts of town is the well-known Little Brown Church in the Vale, whose beauty is captured in the hymn, "The Church in the Wildwood." Despite being known regionally as the site of a picturesque wedding chapel, Nashua has not been able to build upon this strength. For lack of a plan, it has been forced to sit back and watch its young people move to other towns.

That could have been the plight of North Adams, Massachusetts, but town leaders refused to let the town continue on its downward spiral. In the 1950s, the bustling, vibrant city was the Silicon Valley of the electronics era. Its largest employer, Sprague Electric, employed 4,000 people. By the mid 1980s, however, Asian companies began to dominate the electronics industry. Mayor John Barrett remembers the day Sprague left North Adams in 1986: "The president of the company described North Adams as a shrinking, depressing city with no future." Hardly a ringing endorsement for some new company to move into town! According to the 1990 census, North Adams had the second lowest per-capita income in the state.

Barrett and a small group of civic leaders decided to reinvent the town. They didn't know how they would attract new jobs, but they knew something had to be on the horizon. That something was the Internet.

In the 1990s, a North Adams native started Tripod, a company that helped people build their own Web sites. Although Lycos eventually bought this local company, it spawned many new companies in the high-tech field. Among those calling North Adams home is George Gilder, high-tech guru and author of many books, including *Telecosm*, which accurately forecast the burgeoning Internet field. The former Sprague Electric plant has been converted into MASS MoCA, the world's largest Museum of Contemporary Art. Some parts of the old factory have been converted into a digital campus, allowing for the clustering of many high-tech companies looking for lower costs of living and housing.

Feet on the Ground

Three lessons emerge from the stories related above.

Lesson #1: Change Happens. People come and go, companies and industries start up and fade away, prosperity and health can be here one second and gone the next. Relationships and partnerships are forged and broken. Accidents happen; natural disasters occur. New ideas come up, some good, some bad. Some risks pan out, and some don't. Life goes on regardless.

Most things do change—often when you least expect them to.

One town blindsided by change was Charles City, Iowa, which was ripped apart when a tornado moved through a portion of northeastern Iowa in the spring of 1968. The tornado left 13 dead and leveled 256 businesses, 1,250 homes and whole neighborhoods. Townspeople quickly rebuilt the downtown area, retaining its quaintness while making improvements to the business district. And no Floridian will forget the horrific force of Hurricane Andrew, which caused record damage in 1992 to a number of towns along Florida's east coast.

Sometimes change throws you for a loop, even if you're expecting it. So you should not only expect change to happen but also take steps to be proactive and look ahead. Try to forge the change yourself to keep your community healthy and thriving. A community needs people with the foresight to look ahead, to see both good and bad changes coming and to know how to steer toward the good and away from the bad.

You'll need to call on many of the same skills and attributes outlined in the preceding chapters. For instance, you'll need a can-do attitude to keep a positive balance in your community and to make the changes necessary to become or stay healthy. The ability to shape and reshape your community's vision will improve your chances of making change work in your town's favor. And taking an entrepreneurial approach can help a community shift from misfortune to fortune. Don't wait for change to happen; make the right kind of change happen for your town.

Down the Tubes?

Coudersport, a town of 2,600 in the northwestern part of Pennsylvania, was on top of the world until mid-2002. Its raw census data attracted me to the town, and if I just went by the data the town would appear on my list of top agurbs in America (see Appendix A). But numbers don't tell the whole story.

Coudersport was home to Adelphia Communications Corporation, the $3.6-billion annual revenue cable television giant owned by the Rigas family. The company employed more than 2,000 people in the region, and its founder generously funded civic projects ranging from the local hospital to a world-class golf course. In 2002, however, the company edged toward bankruptcy when news came that it had made $2.3 billion in personal loans to the Rigas family. By early 2003, Adelphia had moved its corporate headquarters to Denver, Colorado, creating a bit of panic in the town. In fact, so many homes went on the market at the same time that real estate agents temporarily ran out of "For Sale" signs. The company will most likely be sold or split up, with many of the town's better-paying jobs disappearing, too.

It will be interesting to see the impact of this financial scandal. Will this small town reinvent itself over the next decade or fall by the wayside? Only time will tell.

Lesson #2: Keep Momentum on Your Side. It's much easier to roll a boulder down a hill than to push one up a hill. This has to do with momentum. The only thing gaining momentum when trying to push a boulder uphill is the sweat on your brow.

Gaining momentum—whether moving forward on projects, on town growth or on industry expansion—is crucial in a small town. Why? Because a momentum shift in a small town can be felt from end to end. Lose momentum, and a town's economic forecast can switch from sunny to stormy in amazingly swift time.

For years, Guymon, Oklahoma, has maintained the momentum associated with its Guymon Pioneer Days Rodeo. Held in May, the rodeo is one of the largest events in the Oklahoma panhandle each year and is among the top 10 in prize money on the professional rodeo circuit. The closest interstate to Guymon is 120 miles south, but that doesn't stop the cowboys—and plenty of visitors—from streaming into the town of 10,472. The annual rodeo has an estimated $1.5 million impact on the local economy, with 60 percent of the spectators and contestants being nonresidents.

Like Guymon, communities that prosper have a keen sense of which way the momentum is going and know how to respond when momentum turns against them and threatens their health. Riding momentum is a bit like riding a bucking bronco: You ride it as long as you can, knowing at some point you're likely to be bucked off. A talented minority of riders can stay on the horse. But even those who are bucked off can fare well if they know not only how to ride but also how to land safely so they can ride again.

Lesson #3: Step Up and Take Charge. Every town has doubters and grumblers who can find something wrong with proposed changes. The beauty of a small town is that these curmudgeons can be won over by other townspeople armed with a can-do attitude, good foresight and a plan to become or remain a thriving town.

Enthusiasm—and persistence—have been the hallmark of Tommy Kramer's tenure as economic development director of Durant, Oklahoma. Named by the International Economic Development Council as the 2003 Outstanding New Economic Developer of the Year, Kramer has been instrumental in recruiting and retaining more than $367 million in business investments for the town of 13,549.

Unlike Kramer, curmudgeons have limited, or no, vision. So the health of a town lies in part on how well the more visionary citizens can help the curmudgeons see a better way of doing things. Curmudgeons pledge allegiance to the status quo and can't imagine doing things differently; this mindset has to be overcome with one that is willing to take necessary risks and to adapt to change.

People in Baraboo, Wisconsin, and the surrounding Sauk County could be excused if they have had more than their share of curmudgeons stretching all the way back to 1942. That's when the U.S. government forced families on 85 farms, covering 7,300 acres, to move so it could erect the Badger Army Ammunition Plant. The farmers were paid for the land but not helped in relocating or finding new work. A good dose of bitterness was mixed in with feelings of patriotism for helping the country in its war efforts. (Incidentally, the plant was used for three wars over the years but has since been decommissioned. The goal is to establish a museum to celebrate the heritage of the people and to preserve the history of the area.)

The bitterness in Baraboo didn't last, however. It gave way to thoughtfulness, planning and forward thinking. Baraboo is a prime example of a town that could have gone either way—it could have let itself waste away to nothing, but it chose to rebuild itself. The community drew together, developed a core set of values and principles to spur town growth and health and formed the Sauk County Economic Development Corporation. Since 1960 the population of Baraboo has grown nearly 40 percent, while Sauk County's population has grown nearly 50 percent.

For another example of a take-charge community, look at Paris, Illinois, which suffered the loss of several manufacturing plants in the 1990s. Although Paris is off the beaten track, more than 15 miles from the nearest interstate, a group of citizens came together and decided to use the closed plants as assets. They took the attitude, "If we can get someone to look at these old plants, we'll close the deal to get them here." Numerous times, manufacturers toured the old plants but didn't find them to their liking. What they *did* like was the group's contagious enthusiasm and can-do attitude. Today Paris features a new industrial park full of manufacturing plants that have created many new jobs for local residents.

One Town's Loss is Another's Gain

You probably haven't heard of P.K. Holmes. You won't even find a statue in his honor in his hometown of Newport, Arkansas, where he was a successful businessman. He had an opportunity to leave a legacy for his town. But he blew it. Big time!

In the mid-1940s Holmes leased space to a young man who built a fairly successful small business, which began grossing about $250,000 per year. When the lease came up in 1950, Holmes refused to renew it at any price, bought the franchise from the young man and turned the business over to his son.

The young man, who had naively signed a lease without any renewal options, wanted to move to St. Louis, but his wife insisted that they live in a small town. They moved some 200 miles northwest to Benton County, Arkansas, and started anew. Twelve years later, in 1962, he tried a new concept that quickly caught on.

The young man is, of course, Sam Walton. The company is Wal-Mart. And the town is Bentonville, Arkansas, home to hundreds of local millionaires who used to drive trucks or work as Wal-Mart cashiers, secretaries or store managers before cashing in their stock. Although the company has its share of critics, who believe the opening of a Wal-Mart on the outskirts of a small town often leads to the demise of the downtown shopping area, Wal-Mart has done well by its hometown. In the past 40 years, Bentonville has grown from 3,000 to 19,730 residents, and more than 60,000 new jobs have been created in Benton County. In 2003, the county's unemployment rate was two percent.

In contrast, Newport has grown by only about 800 residents in the last 40 years (its 2000 Census total was 7,811). The number of jobs in the county declined slightly, and the county's unemployment rate in 2003 was nine percent.

By the way, Sam Walton returned to Newport in 1969, to build a Wal-Mart. The store that P.K. Holmes gave his son, after denying a lease extension to Walton, soon closed.

Blending the Keys

Just as one person can really make a difference in a small community, any of the keys to small-town success can make a difference—either for good or for bad. In other words, any key can be the deciding factor in whether a town is headed toward greater vitality and prosperity or toward troubled times.

Each key is important. Each one's presence (a positive) or absence (a negative) can be felt throughout the town. Even the smallest things matter in a rural community and can shift its fortunes one way or the other.

In this way, at least, small towns are more exciting places to live in than big cities. More is at stake each day, and each citizen plays a part. *Everyone* can make a difference in some way. And no matter what their individual talents, ideas or capabilities, *all* citizens can contribute a can-do attitude. When enough people make a positive difference, the town is bound to prosper—and the Teeter-Totter Factor will not strand you in the air but provide an enjoyable ride, with your feet coming down firmly on the ground.

Case Study: Making
All the Keys Work

N   ow that you've read about the 7½ keys that successful small
        towns use to remain healthy and prosperous, you're probably
        wondering, *Does any town put it all together? Does one town truly
excel in each key?*

Certainly, all of the towns mentioned as examples in this book are
doing something right. A great number of them shine in many or most
of the keys. Of course, no town is perfect; every town (and city) faces
limitations and challenges. That said, it's useful to choose one town that
excels in most of the keys and take a closer look at how it operates.

Many towns could have been chosen to showcase as a case study.
Oxford, Mississippi; Columbus, Indiana; Bend, Oregon; Kearney,
Nebraska; Natchitoches, Louisiana; Columbia, Tennessee; Moses Lake,
Washington; Newberry, South Carolina; Dodgeville, Wisconsin; Gillette,
Wyoming; Bowling Green, Kentucky; Morehead City, North Carolina;
and Cape Girardeau, Missouri, were all leading contenders. From that
group, I chose Cape Girardeau, located on the western banks of the
Mississippi River in southeast Missouri.

Why Cape Girardeau? For starters, Cape Girardeau's numbers reflect
growth and prosperity. It is a city on the rise, as evidenced by the figures
in Table 11.1:

**Table 11.1: How Cape Girardeau Compares
to the Nation (1990–2000)**

	Cape Girardeau	National Average
Growth in per-capita income	54%	50%
Change in families living below poverty level	-31%	-8%
Increase in median home value	56%	51%
Residents over age 25 with a bachelor's degree	30%	24%
Increase in percent of residents with a bachelor's degree	6%	4%

While the statistics are impressive, Cape Girardeau is much more than facts and figures. It is a city with a storied past, whose residents are guiding its growth and nurturing its well-being. The following pages give you a closer look at Cape Girardeau and discuss how the city excels, or strives to excel, in each of the 7½ keys.

From Storied Past to Bright Future

In 1931 Dennis Scivally began what is now known as "Ten Mile Garden." Aptly named, the garden stretched along old Highway 61 from Cape Girardeau to Jackson, 10 miles north. By 1939, more than 25,000 rose bushes had been planted—red ones on one side of the highway and white on the other to represent the North and the South in the Civil War. (During the war, Union forces occupied Cape Girardeau and built four forts to protect the town and the river. Today, the town has memorials honoring both the Union and Confederate soldiers.) Soon Cape Girardeau became world-famous for its garden and earned the nickname, "City of Roses on the River." Although the Ten Mile Garden ended in 1963 when work on new Highway 61 began, local residents still maintain more than 20 rose gardens throughout the city.

The Mississippi River is also a significant factor in Cape Girardeau's past and future. The town, founded in 1793, evolved from a small French trading post on the river. By the time the Lewis and Clark Expedition came through the settlement in 1803, more than 1,000 people lived there. The arrival of the steamboat on the Mississippi River in 1835 transformed The Cape, as it's known to local residents, into a river boomtown. It became the busiest port between St. Louis and Memphis. After the Civil War, with the introduction of rail service and the establishment of public education and of Southeast Missouri State in 1873, growth continued. In fact, with the advent of rail service, the town doubled its population in just a few months. Shops opened, hotels went up and the town began booming.

The river has been both boon and bane to Cape Girardeau. Every few years the mighty Mississippi overflows its banks. Flood waters have ravaged The Cape's downtown area many times, wiping out businesses and causing great damage. In 1956 the city began work on a floodwall to protect itself; it took eight years and $4 million to complete, but the project has saved the downtown numerous times.

Today, The Cape has many assets and attractions. It is both a river town and, thanks to Southeast Missouri State University, a college town. It's a garden town and an arts town; in addition to hosting many quilt shows and exhibits, The Cape features numerous murals on its flood wall and downtown walls. With 26 parks and hiking trails close at hand, including the Trail of Tears State Park, and numerous sports facilities, it is an outdoors town. Plus, The Cape employs nearly 7,000 in manufacturing firms and another 2,000 in agriculture. You'll also find service-oriented and information-based workforces in industries as diverse as printing services, apparel, disposable diapers, cement and laminated oak flooring. Cape Girardeau is home to more than 160 manufacturing and wholesaling firms; approximately 1,400 businesses operate within the city.

The town, which numbers many historical buildings among its downtown edifices, also remembers its history. A Cape Girardeau resident designed and created the Missouri state flag. The Common Pleas Courthouse and Courthouse Park mark the site of historic Indian council meetings and served

Slowly but Surely

Cairo, Illinois, used to be the regional center for southwestern Illinois and southeastern Missouri. During the 1940s, however, Cape Girardeau began taking over Cairo's role. By 1950 Cape Girardeau had fully assumed the regional role it maintains today. As you can see from the data in Table 11.2, one city continued to grow while the other stagnated and began a long, downward decline.

Today nearly 150,000 people work in Cape Girardeau and the surrounding area. The city is responsible for one-third of the workforce within a 40-mile radius.

Table 11.2: Comparing Cape Girardeau and Cairo

	Cairo	Cape Girardeau
1900 population	12,566	4,815
1920 population	15,203	10,252
1940 population	14,407	19,426
1960 population	9,348	24,947
1980 population	5,931	34,361
2000 population	3,632	35,349

as headquarters for the Union Provost Marshal during the Civil War. The country's first long-distance phone call west of the Mississippi was made from Cape Girardeau to let merchants in Jackson know that the steamboats had arrived.

Cape Girardeau not only appreciates such past events and places, it looks forward to an ever-brighter future. A new suspension bridge under construction is expected to bear 26,000 cars per day by 2015. Because of the city's businesses and shops, its two full-service hospitals and the university, it's estimated that as many as 90,000 people already find their way to Cape Girardeau every day—to work, shop, attend class and receive medical care. Not bad for a city of fewer than 36,000.

While Cape Girardeau seems to have something for everyone, it still has weaknesses, shortcomings and challenges—like any town does. Although aesthetically pleasing, its rolling hills make it difficult to build large projects. The river forms a natural barrier and forces growth in one direction. The poor section of town continues to decline, and some racial tensions exist. One wealthy businessman is often at odds with the city and has both the money and the willingness to spend it to upend community projects. But the city approaches those challenges in ways that are most likely to help it overcome obstacles and prosper.

Possessing a Can-Do Attitude

Cape Girardeau might be known as the City of Roses on the River, but its second nickname could be "The Can-Do City in the Show-Me State." It has shown a can-do attitude from the time of its namesake, Jean Baptiste Girardot, down through the years through many people and events, including the building of the River Wall to keep the Mississippi River at bay. The 20-foot-high wall stretches for 1.1 miles and has saved the downtown area from untold damage, thus having a significant economic impact on the city.

In addition to building the River Wall, Cape Girardeau offers another example of can-do attitude in action: building the Show Me Center, the home court for the men's and women's basketball teams at Southeast Missouri State University and an entertainment and meeting hub. In the early 1980s, the university wanted to build a new arena to replace its 1930s-era gym, and the city wanted a convention center. People on both sides knew there wasn't enough money to fund two separate projects. So, rather than battle one another for city and state funding, they partnered and sought funding for a building that would suit each party's needs.

Show Me the Money

At a rodeo it hosted, Cape Girardeau's Show Me Center used $2 bills at its ticket office and concession stands to make change for attendees. The idea was to illustrate how the dollars from the center circulate throughout the entire community. Afterward, the center ran a promotion, saying, "If you get a $2 bill, it's due to dollars turning over from the rodeo." Don't think you can't buy anything for $2 anymore: It can buy you great public relations, as it did for the Show Me Center.

The Show Me Center was a $13.5 million project, with $5 million coming from the city, funded by a three percent hotel/motel room tax and a one percent restaurant tax for 20 years. Southeast Missouri State came through with $8.5 million and also built an adjacent student activity center for $3 million.

The project was not without problems. Although a referendum passed overwhelmingly to build the center on Southeast's campus, a local businessman led an effort to move the facility to the west end of town, where most of the hotels are located. The university wanted the center to be on campus so students could walk to classes and sporting events—and to ensure state funding for the project. To stop construction, the businessman filed a lawsuit, which was eventually defeated in the Missouri Supreme Court.

The center opened its doors for business in 1987. It offers 32,000 square feet of exhibit space and numerous meeting rooms, can seat 2,000 for a formal dinner and accommodates 7,200 spectators for athletic contests. Its annual operating budget is $1.1 million. Despite the legal battles and multiple interests of those involved in developing the Show Me Center, the operating agreement between the city and the university is a one-page document that gives priority to the university basketball teams. Beyond that, the facility is to be rented out in the best way possible. By the end of 2002, the Show Me Center had welcomed more than 4.5 million patrons and hosted 6,207 events ranging from rodeos to political rallies, from home and garden shows to athletic camps, from tractor pulls to top-name musical acts, from ice shows to circuses.

"Lots of towns have tried to do what we have done here, but it is difficult to accomplish," says David Ross, director of the Show Me Center. "There was a great deal of political capital expended to get this project done. Somewhat as a result of this project, the mayor of 16 years did not run again, the city manager left six months after the facility was completed, and the university president left for another opportunity within two years." Despite this fallout, the center remains a testament to a city and a university, both with a can-do attitude, that banded together to pull off something that is rarely accomplished between two such entities.

Having a Vision

The good news for The Cape is that its per-capita income and other essential figures are healthy and climbing. Even better news is that the city is spending time on shaping its future to ensure those figures continue to climb. The Cape clearly spells out its vision in its Vision 2020 Strategic Plan, which supplanted a 2000 Strategic Plan generated in 1987. The Vision 2020 Strategic Plan was developed by a special committee that conducted focus groups and gathered information and input from people in local organizations, service clubs and schools, as well as individual residents.

An Early Vision of River Campus

Noted author and native Missourian Mark Twain, who grew up about 230 miles up the river in Hannibal, mentioned Cape Girardeau in his book, *Life on the Mississippi*: "Cape Girardeau is situated on a hillside, and makes a handsome appearance. There is a great Jesuit school for boys at the foot of the town by the river.... There was another college higher up on an airy summit—a bright new edifice, picturesquely and peculiarly towered and pinnacled...."

That "bright new edifice" grew into Southeast Missouri State University; the Jesuit school, formerly known as St. Vincent's Seminary, will become what is now referred to as River Campus: the Southeast Missouri State University School of Visual and Performing Arts. River Campus will also include a regional museum and carries an estimated price tag of $35.6 million. The joint venture is being funded through a partnership involving the city, the university and the state of Missouri.

Upon completion, River Campus—which will consist of renovated historic buildings and new construction—will include not only classrooms, offices and recital halls but also a state-of-the-art performance hall, rehearsal rooms, recording studio, music library, theater, museum exhibit space and art studios. River Campus will add to the arts flavor already present in Cape Girardeau, attracting tourism dollars, acting as a selling point for industries looking to relocate in The Cape and serving as a gateway to the city by way of the new Emerson Memorial Bridge. Thanks to the vision and partnership of the city, university and state, Cape Girardeau promises to keep on rolling, just like the river that borders it.

The Vision 2020 Mission Statement reads, *The City of Cape Girardeau will be a regional center and a great place to visit, live, work and raise a family. Cape Girardeau will be a progressive community that is safe, encourages community involvement and fosters pride and prosperity for all citizens.* This statement acts as a rudder for each of the five main areas of the plan: arts, culture and leisure; community services and enrichment; economic development; education; and transportation and infrastructure. Each of those five areas has a specific mission statement that meshes with the city's overall mission, in addition to specific goals and objectives and "strategies for success" (actions to be taken to realize those goals and objectives).

"We review a five-year plan annually and incorporate the strategic plan into the review process," says Mayor Jay Knudtson. "But, more important, what we do is review the mission statement at our annual retreat and hold ourselves accountable for the past year. We try to grade ourselves on how well we succeeded in fulfilling the components of the mission statement. It is the foundation behind everything we do, just as it should be for any corporation, city or any other entity. We try to be honest with ourselves and truly hold ourselves accountable for how well we perform as a city."

Leveraging Its Resources

The Cape has plenty of resources to leverage and, in part because of its comprehensive and well-thought-out strategic plan, it makes the most of those resources. As a result, outsiders see Cape Girardeau as a multifaceted community with much to offer in education, the arts, the outdoors, technology and manufacturing, to name a few areas.

The Mississippi River gave the town its beginnings, and the characteristics of the river—its relentlessness, durability, ruggedness, power and usefulness—seem to have left their imprint. The river in its untamed state has caused heartache and sorrow in The Cape, but for the greater part it has brought opportunities, commerce and prosperity. In 1975, people from Scott and Cape Counties came together to establish the Southeast Missouri Regional Port Authority (Semo Port), located in nearby Scott City. The two counties approved a ¼-cent sales tax for four years (1986–1990) to generate funds to develop a harbor and a general cargo dock. The referendum passed by more than 70 percent in both counties, raising $7.3 million over the four years.

Today, 15 major barge lines provide service to Cape Girardeau and to the port, which is a major distribution point for petroleum, grain and cement. Semo Port has nearby access to three interstates and to highways, a regional airport and railroad lines. While there has been some disappointment that the harbor hasn't drawn in more business, the port has $17 million in assets and 500 acres of land for development, with 70 acres fully developed. The port also owns its own short-line railroad with six miles of track and switches up to 2,000 cars per year. It has procured $21 million in private investments, creating more than 100 jobs in the process.

Operating Under Sound Leadership

Jay Knudtson was elected mayor of Cape Girardeau in 2002, just 13 years after his job first brought him to the town. He says, "One of the first things I had to do was to get my arms around the finances of the city. The city management had to do its level best to reduce expenses and optimize revenue. And that is a hard decision to make. It requires belt tightening." And it is aided, Knudtson learned, by a culture of leadership that empowers private citizens to make crucial recommendations to the city about its finances.

"I thought we should put together a task force of local, non-politician citizens to look at our finances," Knudtson recalls. "I asked each council member to submit one citizen from his or her particular ward. In the end, we got 12 citizens who represented all walks of life, all races, married and single, blue collar and professional."

This diverse group met several times with the city manager and the city finance director, without any direction from the mayor or city council, and eventually recommended a ¼-cent sales tax, a local use tax on goods or materials purchased from out-of-state companies via catalogs and the Internet, an extension of a 10-cent per one hundred dollar assessed valuation property tax and a storm water utility fee. Together, these recommendations would have raised about $4.1 million to fund city operating expenses, new equipment, storm water projects, construction of a new fire station, expansion and renovation of the police station and a family aquatic center. Voters, however, defeated the proposed tax increases and fees.

But the salient point is that this task force had the power to decide not only how to fund the projects but also how the city should prioritize the projects. This leadership style is one of the reasons that Cape Girardeau has a bright future.

And the Survey Says...

Cape Girardeau extensively surveyed its citizens in 1987, 1994 and 2002 to ascertain how they feel the city is performing in vital areas and to document areas of concern. Some of the findings of the most recent survey, reflecting on the leadership of the city, appear in Table 11.3 (the percentages reflect those who responded Excellent or Good to the questions about the issues):

Table 11.3: Cape Girardeau Survey

Topic	1987	1994	2002
Cape is a progressive community	52%	47%	67%
Effort to attract new business to the area	43%	39%	46%
More family and general practice physicians are needed in Cape	56%	79%	52%
Overall performance of city government	31%	39%	49%
Overall performance of chamber of commerce	54%	50%	57%

Encouraging an Entrepreneurial Approach

John and Jerri Wyman met in Cape Girardeau in the late 1980s while attending Southeast Missouri State University and, after graduation, started a restaurant in a neglected part of downtown. That first restaurant led to several other restaurants, a gourmet food store and extensive remodeling of several older commercial buildings and homes in the downtown area. From the start they had a keen interest in preserving the old downtown area and their vision, says Jerri, is "to make the downtown a place we want to live in and do business in."

Cape Girardeau, through the efforts of the Wymans and other like-minded entrepreneurs and concerned citizens, has vastly improved its downtown since the mid-1990s by adding numerous galleries and restaurants. The Wymans now own 15 downtown properties, seven of which are commercial establishments. They hope to use one rehabbed office building as an incubator to spur new business start-ups in The Cape. Not all of their ventures have succeeded, but the Wymans haven't allowed "bumps in the road" to affect their enthusiasm. They are typical of many entrepreneurs in that, when they fail, they just pick themselves up and keep on going.

The Wymans view the downtown area as a mecca for young people who "want to come back to small towns. They have access to everything," says John. "The growing venues in Cape Girardeau offer them many of the same things they can get in a St. Louis or a Memphis but without the hassles of big city life. The city is screaming for growth and will support it in the long term."

Spoken like a true entrepreneur.

Maintaining Local Control

Gary Rust, now chairman of the board of Rust Communications, bought a 1,500-circulation weekly newspaper in Cape Girardeau in the early 1960s. In the following 35 years, he grew Rust Communications from that one weekly paper to more than 40 newspapers in seven states, with total readership exceeding one million. In the process, he built an organization that is something of an anomaly in the newspaper business: He constructed an independent network of family newspapers, with each paper retaining independence and local control.

In 2001, Rust retired from the daily management of the corporation and handed the reins to two of his sons, Jon and Rex. The company remains headquartered in Cape Girardeau and has contributed substantially to numerous community projects and to Southeast Missouri State University. Rust Communications, for example, has funded literacy programs, used the company's borrowing capacity to guarantee a development fund for the city's chamber of commerce, and sponsored an array of events ranging from ballets to basketball tournaments to Christmas gift drives. The company's community involvement makes a difference not only in Cape Girardeau but also in the other towns in which it owns papers.

"Our newspaper helps define the community," Jon Rust says. "In contrast to a lot of large newspaper companies in small towns, we don't shy away from a strong editorial voice. We delve deeply into difficult issues. And instead of avoiding conflict, which some larger chains feel can jeopardize their franchise in a town, we believe that informed discourse makes for a more vibrant and productive community."

Although it has enjoyed considerable growth over the years, Rust Communications retains its small-town values. Many believe—and Jon Rust is among them—that the existence of family-owned single newspapers in small markets is in peril. But what Rust Communications has done for Cape Girardeau, and for the many other communities in which it owns newspapers, provides a shining example of how maintaining local control can benefit a community.

Showcasing Its Brand

For all that The Cape has going for it—perhaps in part *because* it has so much going for it—it doesn't have much of a brand. Other than being known as a regional center that has much to offer, Cape Girardeau doesn't have a particular brand. Its diverse economic base includes agriculture, manufacturing, medical facilities, retail establishments and a state university.

Paintings on the Walls

For downtown Cape Girardeau, native Margaret Randol Dement designed a colorful mural that depicts 45 famous Missourians. This wall of fame, painted on the Mississippi River flood wall, includes people as diverse as Harry S Truman, Frank and Jesse James, Samuel Clemens (Mark Twain), Rush Limbaugh, Tennessee Williams, T.S. Eliot and Calamity Jane.

Other murals make the downtown unique and beautiful while maintaining a sense of the town's history.

The River Heritage Mural Association, established in the late 1980s, has since completed six outdoor murals and one indoor mural in Cape Girardeau. Plans call for a 1,100-foot mural, which will depict the town's 500-year history, to be painted on the River Wall. The estimated cost of $200,000 will be financed through donations and funding from the downtown merchants association and convention and visitors bureau.

"The murals have played an important role in the business of tourism," says Tim Blattner, president of the River Heritage Mural Association. "They serve as attractions to get people to stop in between St. Louis and Memphis and also are a source of community pride. They are a window into the heart and history of the citizens of Cape. These icons of our past are a source of pride to help bring new people into our community."

Never a city to stand still, Cape Girardeau appears up to the challenge of solving its identity crisis. In the summer of 2003, it commissioned a marketing study to identify a brand the city can sell to tourists. It recognizes the need for a brand and is aggressively going after one.

Balancing on the Teeter-Totter

Cape Girardeau has built several schools in recent years, is developing a state-of-the-art River Campus and is constructing a new bridge to increase traffic flow across the Mississippi. The city still wants to grow, especially in its industries and in job opportunities. It certainly seems headed toward its vision of being a regional center and a great place to visit, live, work and raise a family.

The River Campus project, however, has been a bone of contention for many citizens who question the sagacity of committing so much money to an arts center. Many taxpayers are tired of opening up their wallets and paying higher taxes for some new project. One local businessman who initially supported the development of River Campus took an opposing stance and has had a polarizing effect on the city. Part of The Cape's fortunes for the near future are tied up with this businessman's legacy in the town, and the two seem locked in a love-hate relationship. Nevertheless, the River Campus project is moving ahead despite objections and is scheduled for completion in 2004.

Part of what makes living in a smaller community so exciting is that everything seems to matter. People are passionate about their towns and aren't afraid of speaking their minds. Often, their passions will conflict with other people's passions. Everyone wants the best for his or her town, but viewpoints will differ. The leadership in a small community has to take all of this into account while continuing to press toward the town's collective vision of prosperity.

Little things do matter in a small town like Cape Girardeau. The consequences of decisions both big and small can be felt from one end of the town to the other.

Comparing Agurbs and Cities

T his book has extolled the virtues of agurbs. But how well do they stack up against cities? And how do agurb counties compare to MSA counties?

First, look at how the agurb counties stack up against one another and against similar-sized counties, as well as how they compare to larger counties and to all U.S. counties. The figures in Table 12.1 for population and employment increases are from 1990 to 2000; the per-capita income figures are from 1989 to 1999.

Table 12.1: County Comparison

Area	Population in 2000	Average Population Increase	Average Employment Increase	Average Per-Capita Income Increase
Counties of Top 100 Agurbs	5,151,451	27.9%	32.1%	51.1%
Counties of All 397 Agurbs	16,298,865	19.7%	24.0%	51.0%
Non-MSA Counties, Excluding Agurbs	37,105,585	7.5%	8.3%	47.1%
Non-MSA Counties (2,320)	53,404,450	11.3%	13.1%	48.3%
MSA Counties (822)	220,238,823	17.9%	14.7%	50.0%
All U.S. Counties (3,142)	273,643,273	13.1%	13.8%	50.0%

Consider four points about these figures. First, non-MSA counties—of which agurb counties are a part—on the whole are doing significantly worse than their bigger brethren, MSA counties. Second, the agurb counties—particularly the top 100—separate themselves from both the MSA and other non-MSA counties, especially in population and employment increases. When you exclude the agurbs' counties from the non-MSA counties, the population and employment changes drop to single digits and per-capita income (PCI) drops three percent below the national average.

Third, employment increases have exceeded population increases in the agurb counties much more dramatically than in any other category. This is a prime indicator of health and growth. To illustrate the importance of this correlation, consider MSA counties: the 3.2 percent difference in population growth over job growth equals 7,047,642 more people than jobs.

Fourth, the income in agurbs is better than in other counties. It's about three points better than all non-MSA counties and about one point better than MSA counties and the country as a whole. You can look at the latter difference in two ways: The cost of living is lower in the agurbs and non-MSA counties than it is in MSA counties (though in some small resort towns the cost of living can equal or surpass that of the state's major cities), so the slight percentage increase in income goes farther in an agurb. (See Table 12.2 for comparative incomes between some agurbs and some larger cities.) And many people leave big cities and go to agurbs to upgrade their quality of life, not for the money. That they receive, on average, more for their money in an agurb, is icing on the cake.

Table 12.2: The $100,000 Income Question

Say you live in New York City, Chicago or San Jose (Silicon Valley) and make $100,000 a year. This table shows what you would need to make in various agurbs to maintain the same standard of living you enjoy in the city on your $100,000 income. (This information is based on data gathered from homefair.com on February 26, 2003.)

ST	City	You'd need to make this income to maintain the standard of living that you'd have on $100,000 in NEW YORK CITY	You'd need to make this income to maintain the standard of living that you'd have on $100,000 in CHICAGO	You'd need to make this income to maintain the standard of living that you'd have on $100,000 in SAN JOSE (Silicon Valley)
AL	Fort Payne	$34,902	$53,302	$45,823
AZ	Prescott	38,558	58,886	50,623
AR	Hot Springs	31,899	48,717	41,882
AR	Paragould	31,846	48,635	41,811
CO	Durango	46,415	70,886	60,940
CO	Glenwood Springs	56,979	87,019	74,809
CO	Vail	76,823	117,325	100,863

FL	Vero Beach	30,819	47,067	40,463
GA	Brunswick	30,312	46,292	39,797
GA	Thomasville	32,219	49,204	42,301
ID	Coeur d'Alene	33,333	50,907	43,764
IN	Columbus	34,783	53,120	45,667
IA	Ames	35,467	54,165	46,565
KS	Garden City	35,909	54,841	47,146
KY	Bowling Green	29,305	44,754	38,475
LA	Hammond	32,153	49,105	42,215
MD	Easton	40,622	62,038	53,334
MI	Petoskey	37,251	56,890	48,907
MI	Traverse City	37,985	58,011	49,871
MO	Cape Girardeau	34,706	53,003	45,566
MT	Bozeman	36,639	55,956	48,105
NE	Kearney	36,712	56,068	48,201
NV	Carson City	41,579	63,500	54,590
NH	Concord	40,545	61,921	53,233
NH	Lebanon	43,740	66,800	57,427
NM	Taos	42,529	64,950	55,837
NC	Hendersonville	36,639	55,956	48,105
OK	Durant	31,484	48,083	41,336
OR	Bend	40,491	61,839	53,162
OR	Grants Pass	37,935	57,935	49,806
SC	Georgetown	40,111	61,258	52,662
SC	Hilton Head Island	44,993	68,714	59,072
TN	Greeneville	31,923	48,752	41,912
TX	Eagle Pass	34,390	52,522	45,152
UT	Logan	34,629	52,886	45,465
UT	Park City	43,482	66,406	57,089
UT	St. George	36,067	55,081	47,353
WA	Port Townsend	43,774	66,853	57,472
WY	Gillette	33,537	51,218	44,032
	Average	$38,294	$58,484	$50,278

Now take a look, in Table 12.3, at how the counties of the agurbs stack up against some of the counties containing the nation's bigger cities. This table contains figures for the 10th largest through the 26th largest cities in the United States; their combined population is close to that of the 397 agurb counties. (The 10th through 26th cities represent a better cross-section of the United States. If the list had started with the top-sized cities, it would have only included New York City and Los Angeles to obtain a comparable population figure.) Again, the figures for population and employment increases are from 1990 to 2000; the per-capita income figures are from 1989 to 1999.

The cities (and counties) included here are Detroit (Wayne County), Michigan; San Jose (Santa Clara County), California; Indianapolis (Marion County), Indiana; San Francisco (independent city), California; Jacksonville (Duval County), Florida; Columbus (Franklin County), Ohio; Austin (Travis County), Texas; Baltimore (independent city), Maryland; Memphis (Shelby County), Tennessee; Milwaukee (Milwaukee County), Wisconsin; Boston (Suffolk County), Massachusetts; Washington, D.C. (independent city); El Paso (El Paso County), Texas; Seattle (King County), Washington; Denver (Denver County), Colorado; Nashville (Davidson County), Tennessee; and Charlotte (Mecklenburg County), North Carolina.

Table 12.3: Comparing Agurb and Big City Counties

Area	Population in 2000	Average Population Increase	Average Employment Increase	Average Per-Capita Income Increase
Counties of All 397 Agurbs	16,298,865	19.7%	24.0%	51.0%
Counties of the 10th through 26th largest cities in U.S.	15,625,216	10.4%	9.0%	64.7%

Finally, take a look in Table 12.4 at how the agurbs stack up against three high-tech centers with similar population figures. The high-tech centers are Silicon Valley, California (Santa Clara County); Seattle, Washington (King County); and Boston, Massachusetts (Suffolk and Middlesex Counties). Each of these high-tech centers made the Milken Institute's Top Ten "Tech Poles" List in 1999. (A "tech pole" describes an area with a high concentration of high-tech production.) In fact, San Jose (Silicon Valley) was #1, Boston was

#4, and Seattle-Bellevue-Everett was #5. (Dallas was #2 and Los Angeles was #3. These centers were excluded to obtain a better cross-section of the country and to have comparable population figures.) So you are looking at some of the best high-tech centers in this comparison.

Surprises along the Way

I was surprised to find that 52 of the top 100 agurbs are more than 25 miles from the nearest interstate. As I researched counties and towns and considered all the data in making my selections, I encountered several other surprises, which generally fit into one of three categories:

- I expected college towns to shine, but that often wasn't the case. In fact, I found many college towns to be struggling. Having a college in your town doesn't mean things will automatically go well for the community—and this is tied in part to the community's inability to retain its graduates. Colleges and the communities they're in don't necessarily work together better to retain graduating students or to recruit back past graduates.

- I was mildly surprised to learn of the number of famous people who either hail from small towns or currently live in them. The list includes Tom Brokaw (Yankton, South Dakota), Reba McEntire (Durant, Oklahoma), John Mellencamp (Seymour, Indiana), Oprah Winfrey (Kosciusko, Mississippi), James Jones (Robinson, Illinois), Joe Cocker (Crawford, Colorado), Carl Sandburg (Galesburg, Illinois), Scott Joplin (Sedalia, Missouri), Duncan Hines (Bowling Green, Ohio), James K. Polk (Columbia, Tennessee), Kirsty Alley (Grants Pass, Oregon), Mark Twain (Hannibal, Missouri), Elvis Presley (Tupelo, Mississippi), and Rush Limbaugh (Cape Girardeau, Missouri), to name but a few. Having been home to a celebrity doesn't necessarily mean your town will prosper, but it can help to put it on the map—and, in some cases, attract tourists and fans.

- Another surprise is that the largest city in the county is not always the most prosperous. Examples of smaller towns that are more prosperous than bigger towns within their county include Santa Claus, Indiana; Orrville, Ohio; Camden, Maine; Mackinac Island, Michigan; Buena Vista, Colorado; Nevada City, California; and Spring Hill, Tennessee.

One last observation: Eight agurbs are state capitals. Two are from the Top 100 (Concord, New Hampshire, and Carson City, Nevada). The other six are Juneau, Alaska; Augusta, Maine; Jefferson City, Missouri; Helena, Montana; Pierre, South Dakota; and Montpelier, Vermont.

Table 12.4: Top 100 Agurb Counties vs. Tech-Pole Counties

Area	Population in 2000	Average Population Change	Average Employment Change	Average Per-Capita Income Change
Counties of Top 100 Agurbs	5,151,451	27.9%	32.1%	51.1%
Three Milken Institute Tech-Poles	5,418,006	10.4%	12.2%	75.2%

Note that the positive trends outlined in Tables 12.1, 12.3, and 12.4 regarding employment increase continue. From 2000 to 2003, the Bureau of Labor Statistics shows these percent changes in employment:

- Counties of the Top 100 Agurbs: 6.7 percent increase.
- Counties of all 397 Agurbs: 4.2 percent increase.
- Entire United States: 0.4 percent increase.
- Counties of the 10th through 26th Largest Cities in the US: 2.2 percent decrease.
- Three Milken Institute Tech-Poles: 5.2 percent decrease.

Again, the agurb counties are growing at a significantly higher rate than even these high-tech counties. The per-capita income figures are offset, in most cases, by the higher cost of living in Seattle, Boston and Silicon Valley. In fact, according to homefair.com, if you made a salary of $100,000 in San Jose, you would only have to make an average salary of $50,278 in one of the agurbs listed in Table 12.2. An income of $100,000 in Seattle would equate to $72,728 in the agurbs, and $100,000 in Boston would be comparable to $54,836 in the agurbs. It would be interesting to know how many people left Silicon Valley, Boston or Seattle, for a job in one of the agurbs—and in doing so said goodbye to skyrocketing home prices, property taxes and other indicators of a high cost of living.

Life in an agurb compares quite nicely to life in the big city, especially when you consider cost of living and quality of life issues. Thousands upon thousands of people, tired of the pace, hassle, cost and congestion of larger cities, have fled to the agurbs. Of course, millions more have stayed behind in the big cities, for fine reasons. This isn't an either-or situation. Rather, it's a wake-up call for those who want a different type of life than what is offered in big cities: There are alternatives, and those alternatives can be surprisingly satisfying.

13

A Look into the Agurban Future

The significance of the Third Wave, with about one million people each year moving out of the larger cities, cannot be overstated. This wave has not yet crested and isn't likely to for a long time. In fact, it will likely pick up greater momentum in the years to come, based on a number of factors. Those factors—the same ones that created the wave in the first place—include:

- Improved technology, which opens the door for people to live where they want while still doing the type of work they want, by telecommuting, freelancing or consulting.
- Job outsourcing and business decentralization by companies, which are turning from the large, inner-city factories to newer, smaller, more efficient factories and plants in small towns.
- Decreased transportation and shipping costs, making it less essential for businesses to be located close to their customers or to the axis of communication and travel links, such as a river, railroad or interstate.
- Improvements in communications and travel.
- Deregulation of various industries, including the airlines, telecommunications and trucking industries.
- Globalization, which favors companies that are willing and able to downsize, adapt and embrace new technologies to increase productivity and service—and which prompts more companies to base headquarters or satellite operations in small towns.
- A ready and willing labor force in small towns, which makes for an ideal marriage with companies looking to relocate to smaller communities.
- Lower costs of operating a business in a small town.
- Lower cost of living in small towns.
- A variety of quality of life issues.

Considered together, these factors make for a convincing argument that the Third Wave will continue long into the future and will increase in size, rather than decrease. More businesses are looking to smaller communities for many of the reasons listed above, and more people have a real choice in whom they want to work for and where they want to live while they work. This wave takes advantage of existing opportunities in small towns and also creates new opportunities, thus perpetuating itself.

Town growth means new construction, so it's not surprising that many small towns are experiencing housing and real estate booms. See Table 13.1 for housing unit comparisons.

Table 13.1: Growth in Number of Housing Units, 1990–2000

United States	20.5%
MSAs	19.9%
Non-MSAs	22.7%
3 Milken Institute Tech-Poles	12.4%
All Agurbs	29.2%
Top 100 Agurbs	34.6%

Town growth also means either new or additional services are needed. Population growth stimulates job growth to meet the needs of the residents. Towns that embrace technology and growth, are aggressive and smart and follow the keys outlined in this book are destined to become the booming towns of the nation. They will remain small, of course, in comparison to cities. But they are now and will continue to be, for Baby Boomers and a growing number of Gen-Xers, the hot spots to live in.

Not For Everyone

The decision to live in a small town is no longer an either-or choice. It's not "*Either* I live in a small community and enjoy the quality of life there, but lose in terms of my employment, *or* I find a great job but lose in terms of where I really want to live." This ability to "have your cake and eat it too"—while living in a small town—continues to expand to more industries as technology opens up opportunities for more people to either work in small towns or to telecommute. This Third Wave will be neither short-lived nor a passing fad; it will remain, and continue to change the face of America, long into the future.

That's not to say that small towns are for everyone; they're not. Living in a small town doesn't automatically mean your life will improve or that you will be happier, more fulfilled and more productive. Those issues are up to you, wherever you choose to live. A small town has its downsides: a more limited culture, at least in terms of its diversity; smaller wages and salaries than those typically found in big cities (though cost of living is also less); more limited social programs and services; and so on.

Then there is the well-documented "Peyton Place" factor: You're under a microscope in a small town. You get to know lots of people and become connected to the town's doings in a variety of ways, but you have to be comfortable with the fact that there are no secrets. In a small town, everyone seems to know everything about everyone else. Privacy is at a premium. If you're a private person, and prefer to keep to yourself, chances are you'll suffer some degree of discomfort in a small town.

Not everyone in a city or a suburb should pack his or her bags and head toward a small town tomorrow. But the opportunity to do so has never been greater and, for the right person, it is an opportunity of a lifetime. Those who prefer the slower pace and the type of life that smaller communities offer— and who don't mind the downsides of small-town life—now have a greater choice than ever in becoming a part of a small town while still working at the job they are best suited for.

The Future Depends on You

The future of small-town America rests solely on the shoulders of the people in those towns. There's no doubt that towns must overcome formidable challenges in order to grow: lack of resources, financial institutions that are controlled from thousands of miles away, industries that are drying up, locations that are less than ideal and climates that are less than conducive to drawing tourists and businesses. Many communities face *all* of these challenges at the same time.

Note that these challenges are not really controllable; that is, you can't change them just through desire and work. But you can plan to succeed *despite* these challenges, minimizing their impact on your community and maximizing your success in the areas you can control: attitude, vision, leadership, entrepreneurial approach, calculated risk-taking and building a brand for your town. The towns that focus on what they can control and take the "Eagle" approach described in Chapter 3—being visionary, bold and courageous— will thrive. Eagle towns attract people and companies looking for better ways to live and better places to live in. They keep in step with technology, using it not to break from their past but to build a bridge to their future.

A bright future for small towns is attainable. Towns that don't adhere to the 7½ keys and don't pay attention to the factors that have resulted in the Third Wave are swiftly being left behind. Those that are adept at using the keys and understand the factors that facilitate small-town prosperity are growing into the boomtowns of America.

One of this book's central themes is the ability of an individual to make a difference in a small community. As Baby Boomers age, they want to make a difference and find a meaning in their lives that stretches beyond material possessions and financial wealth. In a small town, many of them can find that slower pace, a greater connectedness with their neighbors and a feeling that they can make a real difference.

Is a small town the only place where people can find a more meaningful, more satisfying life? Not at all. But for many people a small town is part of a natural progression. The allure and excitement of a big city gives way to the need to dig in, take root and grow in a place that is less jungle and more garden. Small-town America is beckoning many people. But not just *any* small town: boomtowns. The agurbs.

Agurban Life: a Win-Win Proposition

Living in the agurbs is a win-win proposition for people and companies alike—if they both are willing to invest in the towns they inhabit. Companies that relocate in agurbs win for all the reasons previously documented, including lower operating costs, decreased shipping and transportation costs, a ready and willing labor force and improved communications and travel. People who relocate to agurbs win because of lower housing costs and property taxes, lower costs of living, lower crime rates and generally a better environment in terms of air and water quality.

Small towns in America are at a crossroads. They have become the land of opportunity for thousands of companies and millions of people—but a rather sharp divide has materialized between the haves and the have-nots. The great majority of small towns in this country belong to the latter group: the have-nots. Yet there is no other time in American history when they better stand to prosper, based on external factors that continue to facilitate their growth and flourishing.

The vast majority of the prospering small towns in this country—the agurbs—have set themselves apart by excelling in the 7½ keys. Those keys have been the ticket to their success.

Agurbs in the U.S.A.

I n the course of my work, I came across some towns that stood out as "diamonds in the rough" among the more than 15,800 or so small towns across America. In my desire to more fully understand why some communities were growing and offering opportunities to their young people, while others were turning into ghost towns, the idea for this book was born—and with it, the idea for identifying the best small towns in America.

The Selection Method

Based on a number of criteria, I selected the country's top small communities and then narrowed the list to what I call the "Golden Eagles Top 100 Agurbs." The process of selecting the top small towns was neither easy nor swift. The first criterion was that the town had to be from a non-MSA county. (Remember, an MSA is a Metropolitan Statistical Area that has at least one city exceeding 50,000 in population or is an urbanized area defined by the U.S. Census Bureau as having at least 50,000 inhabitants with a total metropolitan population of at least 100,000.) Of the 3,142 counties in the United States, 2,320 are non-MSA counties.

The second criterion centered on county census statistics. To remain in consideration, the county had to show growth in population or employment and per-capita income. If a county's numbers are on the rise, it makes sense that something is going right in at least some of the towns within those counties.

Next, I enlisted the help of the state economic development divisions, asking them to recommend any counties that weren't on my list, based on the first two criteria. Once I received the responses, I had a list of 1,231 counties—in other words, I had eliminated nearly half the potential agurb counties. I researched these counties in more detail. Based on the responses from an initial survey as well as our research, I narrowed the list to 771 counties. I then sent a second, more detailed survey to various entities representing those counties, including chambers of commerce, economic developers, mayors and city or town managers.

Census Bureau Redefines MSAs

On December 27, 2000, the Office of Management and Budget (OMB) announced in the *Federal Register* the adoption of new standards for defining Metropolitan and Micropolitan Statistical Areas. The OMB will apply the new standards with Census 2000 data and announced definitions of areas based on these standards in mid-2003. At this time, an MSA will be based on an urbanized area of 50,000 or more population.

An urbanized area is defined as a statistical geographic entity consisting of a central place, usually a city, and an adjacent, densely settled territory that together contain at least 50,000 people, generally with an overall population density of at least 1,000 people per square mile. Therefore, a city, even with a population under 50,000, may be determined to be an MSA if the area immediately surrounding the city is densely populated.

Based on this new definition, 25 of our 397 agurbs became MSAs, even though only three central cities grew to more than 50,000 in population. I completed my research on the 397 agurbs before the new definitions were announced. As my staff and I continue to look for new communities that may become agurbs, we will follow our definition of an agurb, which is, first and foremost, a prospering rural town with a population under 50,000.

This second survey focused on the 7½ keys and gave the communities a chance to describe how they have used those keys to achieve growth and success. From this survey, from the statistical information I had on the counties and towns and from the exhaustive research and interviewing that my staff and I conducted, I selected the list of 397 agurbs.

From this list I identified the top 100 by delving deeply into quality of life issues as evidenced by the surveys, town Web sites, countless interviews and analyses of how well the towns used the 7½ keys. I chose the top 100 based on measurable benchmarks of success and on perceived indicators of how closely a town's success correlated with its use of the 7½ keys.

Besides the 7½ keys, I considered the following factors and issues in selecting the top agurbs:
- Healthcare
- Education
- Recreation
- Culture

- Taxes
- Cost of living
- Crime rate
- Environment
- Climate
- Airport, highway and interstate access

Golden Eagle Top 100 Agurbs

The Top 100 Agurbs—the Golden Eagles—are the *crème de la crème* of small towns in America. They not only excel in most of the 7½ keys but also have much to offer in a number of other critical areas that impact a town's quality of life. These areas include healthcare, education, recreation, culture, taxes, cost of living, crime rate, environment, climate and access to transportation (airport, highway and interstate). These Top 100 Agurbs consistently rated higher than the other 297 statistically and in how they employ the 7½ keys to fuel their success.

Here are the Top 100 Agurbs, listed in Tables 1 to 6, by region.

Table 1: Golden Eagles East

State	Agurbs (2000 population)	County
MD	Easton (11,708)	Talbot
MD	Ocean City (7,173)	Worcester
ME	Blue Hill (2,390)	Hancock
ME	Camden (3,934)	Knox
ME	Sanford (20,806)	York
NH	Concord (40,687)	Merrimack
NH	Lebanon (12,568);	Grafton
PA	E. Stroudsburg (9,888)	Monroe
VA	Harrisonburg (40,468)	(Independent City)
VA	Rocky Mount (4,066)	Franklin
VT	Stowe (4,339)	Lamoille
WV	Berkeley Springs (663)	Morgan
WV	Moorefield (2,375)	Hardy

Table 2: Golden Eagles Southeast

State	Agurbs (2000 population)	County
AL	Clanton (7,800)	Chilton
AL	Eufaula (13,908)	Barbour
AL	Ft. Payne (12,938)	DeKalb
FL	Apalachicola (2,334)	Franklin
FL	Sopchoppy (426)	Wakulla
FL	Vero Beach (17,705)	Indian River
GA	Brunswick (15,600)	Glynn
GA	Dawsonville (619)	Dawson
GA	Douglas (10,639)	Coffee
GA	Thomasville (18,162)	Thomas
MS	Oxford (11,756)	Lafayette
MS	Philadelphia (7,303)	Neshoba
MS	Picayune (10,535)	Pearl River
NC	Hendersonville (10,420)	Henderson
NC	Highlands (909)	Macon
NC	Morehead City (7,691)	Carteret
SC	Hilton Head Island (33,862)	Beaufort
SC	Georgetown (8,950)	Georgetown
SC	Newberry (10,580)	Newberry
TN	Spring Hill (7,715)	Maury
TN	Crossville (8,981)	Cumberland
TN	Greenville (15,198)	Greene

Table 3: Golden Eagles Midwest

State	Agurbs (2000 population)	County
IA	Ames (50,731)	Story
IL	Marion (16,035)	Williamson
IN	Columbus (39,059)	Bartholomew
IN	Greencastle (9,880)	Putnam
KY	Bardstown (10,374)	Nelson
KY	Bowling Green (49,296)	Warren
MI	Hastings (7,095)	Barry
MI	Petoskey (6,080)	Emmet
MI	Mackinac Island (523)	Mackinac
MI	Traverse City (14,532)	Grand Traverse

State	Agurbs (2000 population)	County
MO	Branson (6,050)	Taney
MO	Camdenton (2,779)	Camden
MO	Cape Girardeau (35,349)	Cape Girardeau
OH	Millersburg (3,326)	Holmes
OH	Waverly (4,433)	Pike
WI	Baraboo (10,711)	Sauk
WI	Dodgeville (4,220)	Iowa
WI	Clintonville (4,736)	Waupaca
WI	St. Croix Falls (2,033)	Polk
WI	Whitewater (13,437)	Walworth

Table 4: Golden Eagles Great Plains

State	Agurbs (2000 population)	County
CO	Durango (13,922)	La Plata
CO	Glenwood Springs (7,736)	Garfield
CO	Buena Vista (2,195)	Chaffee
CO	Telluride (2,221)	San Miguel
CO	Vail (4,531)	Eagle
KS	Garden City (28,451)	Finney
KS	Liberal (19,666)	Seward
MT	Bozeman (27,509)	Gallatin
MT	Kalispell (14,223	Flathead
NE	Kearney (27,431)	Buffalo
WY	Gillette (19,646)	Campbell
WY	Jackson (8,647)	Teton

Table 5: Golden Eagles Southwest

State	Agurbs (2000 population)	County/Parish
AR	Hot Springs (35,750)	Garland
AR	Mountain Home (11,012)	Baxter
AR	Paragould (22,017)	Greene
AZ	Prescott (33,938)	Yavapai
AZ	Tombstone (1,504)	Cochise
LA	Hammond (17,639)	Tangipahoa
LA	Natchitoches (17,865)	Natchitoches

State	Agurbs (2000 population)	County/Parish
NM	Ruidoso (7,698)	Lincoln
NM	Taos (4,700)	Taos
OK	Durant (13,549)	Bryan
OK	Guymon (10,472)	Texas
TX	Marble Falls (4,959)	Burnet
TX	Decatur (5,201)	Wise
TX	Eagle Pass(22,413)	Maverick
TX	Hillsboro (8,232)	Hill
TX	Rockport (7,385)	Aransas

Table 6: Golden Eagles West

State	Agurbs (2000 population)	County
CA	Nevada City (3,001)	Nevada
CA	San Juan Bautista (1,549)	San Benito
ID	Coeur d'Alene (34,514)	Kootenai
ID	Sun Valley (1,427)	Blaine
ID	Sandpoint (6,835)	Bonner
NV	Carson City (52,457)	Independent City
OR	Bend (52,029)	Deschutes
OR	Grants Pass (23,003)	Josephine
UT	Ephraim (4,505)	Sanpete
UT	Logan (42,670)	Cache
UT	Park City (7,371)	Summit
UT	St. George (49,663)	Washington
WA	Clarkston (7,337)	Asotin
WA	Colville (4,988)	Stevens
WA	Friday Harbor (1,989)	San Juan
WA	Moses Lake (14,953)	Grant
WA	Port Townsend (8,334)	Jefferson

Agurb Winners

The following agurbs excelled in the 7½ keys and in the aforementioned quality of life issues. They are among the top 2.5 percent of all non-metro towns in the nation. As with the Top 100, the agurbs are categorized by region (with the Golden Eagles highlighted in bold).

Table 7: Agurbs East

State	Agurbs (2000 population)	County
MA	North Adams (14,681)	Berkshire
MD	Chestertown (4,746)	Kent
MD	**Easton (11,708)**	**Talbot**
MD	Leonardtown (1,896)	St. Mary's
MD	**Ocean City (7,173)**	**Worcester**
MD	Salisbury (23,743)	Wicomico
ME	Belfast (6,381)	Waldo
ME	**Blue Hill (2,390)**	**Hancock**
ME	New Gloucester (4,803)	Cumberland
ME	**Camden (3,934)**	**Knox**
ME	Rumford (6,472)	Oxford
ME	**Sanford (20,806)**	**York**
ME	Waterville (15,605)	Kennebec
ME	Wiscasset (3,603)	Lincoln
NH	**Concord (40,687)**	**Merrimack**
NH	Keene (22,563)	Cheshire
NH	**Lebanon (12,568)**	**Grafton**
NY	Corning (6,426)	Steuben
NY	Lake Placid (2,638)	Essex
NY	Ithaca (29,287)	Tompkins
NY	Cooperstown (2,032)	Otsego
PA	**E. Stroudsburg (9,888)**	**Monroe**
PA	Lewisburg (5,620)	Union
PA	Wellsboro (3,328)	Tioga
VA	Blacksburg (39,573)	Montgomery
VA	**Harrisonburg (40,468)**	**(Independent City)**
VA	Middletown (1,015)	Frederick
VA	**Rocky Mount (4,066)**	**Franklin**

State	Agurbs (2000 population)	County
VT	Brattleboro (12,005)	Windham
VT	Middlebury (8,183)	Addison
VT	Montpelier (8,035)	Washington
VT	**Stowe (4,339)**	**Lamoille**
VT	White River Junction (2,569)	Windsor
WV	**Berkeley Springs (663)**	**Morgan**
WV	**Moorefield (2,375)**	**Hardy**
WV	Morgantown (26,809)	Monongalia
WV	Oak Hill (7,589)	Fayette

Table 8: Agurbs Southeast

State	Agurbs (2000 population)	County
AL	Brewton (5,498)	Escambia
AL	**Clanton (7,800)**	**Chilton**
AL	Cullman (13,995)	Cullman
AL	Double Springs (1,003)	Winston
AL	**Eufaula (13,908)**	**Barbour**
AL	**Ft. Payne (12,938)**	**DeKalb**
AL	Greensboro (2,731)	Hale
AL	Russellville (8,971)	Franklin
AL	Scottsboro (14,762)	Jackson
AL	Talladega (15,143)	Talladega
FL	**Apalachicola (2,334)**	**Franklin**
FL	Bronson (964)	Levy
FL	Chipley (3,592)	Washington
FL	Clewiston (6,460)	Hendry
FL	De Funiak Springs (5,089)	Walton
FL	Key West (25,478)	Monroe
FL	Lake City (9,980)	Columbia
FL	Moore Haven (1,635)	Glades
FL	Okeechobee (5,376)	Okeechobee
FL	**Sopchoppy (426)**	**Wakulla**
FL	**Vero Beach (17,705)**	**Indian River**
GA	Blairsville (659)	Union
GA	Blue Ridge (1,210)	Fannin
GA	**Brunswick (15,600)**	**Glynn**
GA	Calhoun (10,667)	Gordon
GA	Dalton (27,912)	Whitfield

State	Agurbs (2000 population)	County
GA	**Dawsonville (619)**	**Dawson**
GA	**Douglas (10,639)**	**Coffee**
GA	Eatonton (6,764)	Putnam
GA	Hinesville (30,392)	Liberty
GA	Jackson (3,934)	Butts
GA	Jefferson (3,825)	Jackson
GA	Lavonia (1,827)	Franklin
GA	Monticello (2,428)	Jasper
GA	Moultrie (14,387)	Colquitt
GA	Nahunta (930)	Brantley
GA	St. Mary's (13,761)	Camden
GA	Statesboro (22,698)	Bulloch
GA	Thomaston (9,411)	Upson
GA	**Thomasville (18,162)**	**Thomas**
GA	Gainesville (25,578)	Hall
MS	Collins (2,683)	Covington
MS	Forest (5,987)	Scott
MS	Kosciusko (7,372)	Attala
MS	Lucedale (2,458)	George
MS	**Oxford (11,756)**	**Lafayette**
MS	**Philadelphia (7,303)**	**Neshoba**
MS	**Picayune (10,535)**	**Pearl River**
MS	Pontotoc (5,253)	Pontotoc
MS	Starkville (21,869)	Oktibbeha
MS	Tupelo (34,211)	Lee
MS	Vicksburg (26,407)	Warren
NC	Boone (13,472)	Watauga
NC	Brevard (6,789)	Transylvania
NC	Columbus (992)	Polk
NC	Dunn (9,196)	Harnett
NC	Edenton (5,394)	Chowan
NC	Elizabethtown (3,698)	Bladen
NC	**Hendersonville (10,420)**	**Henderson**
NC	**Highlands (909)**	**Macon**
NC	Kitty Hawk (2,991	Dare
NC	Mooresville (18,823)	Iredell
NC	**Morehead City (7,691)**	**Carteret**
NC	Murphy (1,568)	Cherokee

State	Agurbs (2000 population)	County
NC	New Bern (23,128)	Craven
NC	Oxford (8,338)	Granville
NC	Pinehurst (9,706)	Moore
NC	Sanford (23,220)	Lee
NC	Sylva (2,435)	Jackson
NC	Wilkesboro (3,159)	Wilkes
NC	Wilson (44,405)	Wilson
SC	Abbeville (5,840)	Abbeville
SC	**Hilton Head Island (33,862)**	**Beaufort**
SC	Cheraw (5,524)	Chesterfield
SC	**Georgetown (8,950)**	**Georgetown**
SC	**Newberry (10,580)**	**Newberry**
SC	Orangeburg (12,765)	Orangeburg
SC	Ridgeland (2,518)	Jasper
TN	Cleveland (37,192)	Bradley
TN	**Spring Hill (7,715)**	**Maury**
TN	Cookeville (23,923)	Putnam
TN	**Crossville (8,981)**	**Cumberland**
TN	Fairview (5,800)	Scott
TN	**Greenville (15,198)**	**Greene**
TN	La Follette (7,926)	Campbell
TN	Lexington (7,393)	Henderson
TN	Lynchburg (5,740)	Moore
TN	Newport (7,242)	Cocke
TN	Paris (9,763)	Henry
TN	Pulaski (7,871)	Giles
TN	Rutledge (1,187)	Grainger
TN	Sweetwater (5,586)	Monroe
TN	Tazewell (2,165)	Claiborne

Table 9: Agurbs Midwest

State	Agurbs (2000 population)	County
IA	**Ames (50,731)**	**Story**
IA	Hawarden (2,478)	Sioux
IA	Marengo (2,535)	Iowa
IA	Mason City (29,172)	Cerro Gordo
IA	Newton (15,579)	Jasper
IA	Osceola (4,629)	Clarke

State	Agurbs (2000 population)	County
IA	Pella (9,832)	Marion
IA	Spirit Lake (4,261)	Dickinson
IA	Winterset (4,768)	Madison
IL	Danville (33,904)	Vermilion
IL	Effingham (12,384)	Effingham
IL	Galena (3,460)	Jo Daviess
IL	Galesburg (33,709)	Knox
IL	**Marion (16,035)**	**Williamson**
IL	Mattoon (18,291)	Coles
IL	Mt. Vernon (16,269)	Jefferson
IL	Nauvoo (1,063)	Hancock
IL	Paris (9,077)	Edgar
IL	Peru (9,835)	La Salle
IL	Quincy (40,366)	Adams
IL	Robinson (6,822)	Crawford
IL	Tuscola (4,448)	Douglas
IN	Brookville (2,652)	Franklin
IN	**Columbus (39,059)**	**Bartholomew**
IN	**Greencastle (9,880)**	**Putnam**
IN	Greensburg (10,260)	Decatur
IN	Jasper (12,100)	Dubois
IN	Kendallville (9,616	Noble
IN	Lagrange (2,919)	Lagrange
IN	Nashville (825)	Brown
IN	North Vernon (6,515)	Jennings
IN	Princeton (8,175)	Gibson
IN	Santa Claus (2,041)	Spencer
IN	Seymour (18,101)	Jackson
IN	Tell City (7,845)	Perry
IN	Warsaw (12,415)	Kosciusko
KY	Albany (2,220)	Clinton
KY	**Bardstown (10,374)**	**Nelson**
KY	**Bowling Green (49,296)**	**Warren**
KY	Elizabethtown (22,542)	Hardin
KY	Glasgow (13,019)	Barren
KY	Lancaster (3,734)	Garrard
KY	Lebanon (5,718)	Marion
MI	Ahmeek (157)	Keweenaw

State	Agurbs (2000 population)	County
MI	Big Rapids (10,849)	Mecosta
MI	Cadillac (10,000)	Wexford
MI	Charlevoix (2,994)	Charlevoix
MI	Cheboygan (5,295)	Cheboygan
MI	Coldwater (12,697)	Branch
MI	Gaylord (3,681)	Otsego
MI	Greilickville (1,415)	Leelanau
MI	**Hastings (7,095)**	**Barry**
MI	Ludington (8,357)	Mason
MI	Mount Pleasant (25,946)	Isabella
MI	**Petoskey (6,080)**	**Emmet**
MI	Sault St. Marie (16,542)	Chippewa
MI	**Mackinac Island (523)**	**Mackinac**
MI	**Traverse City (14,532)**	**Grand Traverse**
MI	West Branch (1,926)	Ogemaw
MN	Alexandria (8,820)	Douglas
MN	Bemidji (11,917)	Beltrami
MN	Brainerd (13,178)	Crow Wing
MN	Dodge Center (2,226)	Dodge
MN	Fergus Falls (13,471)	Otter Tail
MN	Grand Marsais (1,353)	Cook
MN	Hutchinson (13,080)	McLeod
MN	Park Rapids (3,276)	Hubbard
MN	Pine City (3,043)	Pine
MN	Red Wing (16,116)	Goodhue
MN	Walker (1,069)	Cass
MN	Winona (27,069)	Winona
MO	**Branson (6,050)**	**Taney**
MO	**Camdenton (2,779)**	**Camden**
MO	**Cape Girardeau (35,349)**	**Cape Girardeau**
MO	Farmington (13,924)	St. Francois
MO	Hannibal (17,757)	Marion
MO	Jefferson City (39,636)	Cole
MO	Kimberling City (2,253)	Stone
MO	Lebanon (12,155)	Laclede
MO	Monett (7,396)	Barry
MO	Rolla (16,367)	Phelps
MO	Sedalia (20,339)	Pettis

State	Agurbs (2000 population)	County
MO	Ste. Genevieve (4,476)	Ste. Genevieve
MO	West Plains (10,866)	Howell
OH	Celina (10,303)	Mercer
OH	Chillicothe (21,796)	Ross
OH	Findley (38,967)	Hancock
OH	**Millersburg (3,326)**	**Holmes**
OH	Orrville (8,551)	Wayne
OH	Van Wert (10,690)	Van Wert
OH	**Waverly (4,433)**	**Pike**
OH	Wilmington (11,921)	Clinton
WI	Arbor Vitae (3,153)	Vilas
WI	**Baraboo (10,711)**	**Sauk**
WI	Beaver Dam (15,169)	Dodge
WI	**Dodgeville (4,220)**	**Iowa**
WI	Fond du Lac (42,203)	Fond du Lac
WI	Grantsburg (1,369)	Burnett
WI	Hayward (2,129)	Sawyer
WI	Menominie (14,937)	Dunn
WI	**Clintonville (4,736)**	**Waupaca**
WI	Rhinelander (7,735)	Oneida
WI	Shell Lake (1,309)	Washburn
WI	**St. Croix Falls (2,033)**	**Polk**
WI	Stevens Point (24,551)	Portage
WI	Sturgeon Bay (9,437)	Door
WI	Waterloo (3,259)	Jefferson
WI	**Whitewater (13,437)**	**Walworth**

Table 10: Agurbs Great Plains

State	Agurbs (2000 population)	County
CO	Crested Butte (1,529)	Gunnison
CO	Breckenridge (2,408)	Summit
CO	Central City (515)	Gilpin
CO	Cortez (7,977)	Montezuma
CO	Creede (377)	Mineral
CO	Delta (6,400)	Delta
CO	**Durango (13,922)**	**La Plata**
CO	Elizabeth (1,434)	Elbert

State	Agurbs (2000 population)	County
CO	**Glenwood Springs (7,736)**	**Garfield**
CO	Hot Sulphur Springs (521)	Grand
CO	Montrose (12,344)	Montrose
CO	Pagosa Springs (1,591)	Archuleta
CO	**Buena Vista (2,195)**	**Chaffee**
CO	Steamboat Springs (9,815)	Routt
CO	**Telluride (2,221)**	**San Miguel**
CO	**Vail (4,531)**	**Eagle**
KS	Abilene (6,543)	Dickinson
KS	Alma (797)	Wabaunsee
KS	Dodge City (25,176)	Ford
KS	**Garden City (28,451)**	**Finney**
KS	**Liberal (19,666)**	**Seward**
KS	McPherson (13,770)	McPherson
KS	Salina (45,679)	Saline
MT	**Bozeman (27,509)**	**Gallatin**
MT	Columbus (1,748)	Stillwater
MT	Hamilton (3,705)	Ravalli
MT	Helena (25,780)	Lewis and Clark
MT	**Kalispell (14,223)**	**Flathead**
MT	Livingston (6,851)	Park
MT	Red Lodge (2,177)	Carbon
MT	Townsend (1,867)	Broadwater
ND	Minot (36,567)	Ward
ND	Rolla (1,417)	Rolette
NE	Grand Island (42,940)	Hall
NE	**Kearney (27,431)**	**Buffalo**
NE	Norfolk (23,516)	Madison
NE	Sidney (6,282)	Cheyenne
SD	Aberdeen (24,658)	Brown
SD	Brookings (18,504)	Brookings
SD	Elk Point (1,714)	Union
SD	Pierre (13,876)	Hughes
SD	Sturgis (6,442)	Meade
SD	Watertown (20,237)	Codington
SD	Yankton (13,528)	Yankton
WY	Buffalo (3,900)	Johnson
WY	Cody (8,835)	Park

State	Agurbs (2000 population)	County
WY	**Gillette (19,646)**	**Campbell**
WY	**Jackson (8,647)**	**Teton**
WY	Lander (6,867)	Fremont
WY	Sheridan (15,804)	Sheridan

Table 11: Agurbs Southwest

State	Agurbs (2000 population)	County/Parish
AR	Arkadelphia (10,912)	Clark
AR	Clarksville (7,719)	Johnson
AR	Clinton (2,283)	Van Buren
AR	Harrison (12,152)	Boone
AR	**Hot Springs (35,750)**	**Garland**
AR	Mena (5,637)	Polk
AR	Mount Ida (981)	Montgomery
AR	**Mountain Home (11,012)**	**Baxter**
AR	Mountain View (2,876)	Stone
AR	Murfreesboro (1,764)	Pike
AR	**Paragould (22,017)**	**Greene**
AR	Russellville (23,682)	Pope
AR	Searcy (18,928)	White
AZ	Eagar (4,033)	Apache
AZ	Globe (7,486)	Gila
AZ	**Prescott (33,938)**	**Yavapai**
AZ	**Tombstone (1,504)**	**Cochise**
AZ	Snowflake (4,460)	Navajo
AZ	Thatcher (4,022)	Graham
LA	**Hammond (17,639)**	**Tangipahoa**
LA	**Natchitoches (17,865)**	**Natchitoches**
LA	New Iberia (32,623)	Iberia
LA	Oakdale (8,137)	Allen
LA	Plaquemine (7,064)	Iberville
NM	Espanola (9,688)	Rio Arriba
NM	Estancia (1,584)	Torrance
NM	Farmington (37,844)	San Juan
NM	Gallup (20,209)	McKinley
NM	Grants (8,806)	Cibola
NM	Las Vegas (14,565)	San Miguel

State	Agurbs (2000 population)	County/Parish
NM	**Ruidosa (7,698)**	**Lincoln**
NM	Silver City (10,545)	Grant
NM	**Taos (4,700)**	**Taos**
NM	Truth or Consequences (7,289)	Sierra
OK	**Durant (13,549)**	**Bryan**
OK	**Guymon (10,472)**	**Texas**
OK	Jay (2,482)	Delaware
OK	Madill (3,410)	Marshall
OK	Pryor (8,659)	Mayes
OK	Stillwater (39,065)	Payne
OK	Stilwell (3,276)	Adair
TX	**Marble Falls (4,959)**	**Burnet**
TX	Corsicana (24,485)	Navarro
TX	**Decatur (5,201)**	**Wise**
TX	**Eagle Pass (22,413)**	**Maverick**
TX	**Hillsboro (8,232)**	**Hill**
TX	Jasper (8,247)	Jasper
TX	Kerrville (20,425)	Kerr
TX	Llano (3,325)	Llano
TX	Mt. Pleasant (13,935)	Titus
TX	Pleasanton (8,266)	Atascosa
TX	**Rockport (7,385)**	**Aransas**
TX	Shepherd (2,029)	San Jacinto
TX	Stephenville (14,921)	Erath
TX	Uvalde (14,929)	Uvalde

Table 12: Agurbs West

State	Agurbs (2000 population)	County
AK	Dillingham (2,466)	Dillingham Census Area
AK	Juneau (30,711)	Juneau Borough
AK	North Pole (1,570)	Southeast Fairbanks Census Area
CA	Colusa (5,402)	Colusa
CA	Eureka (26,128)	Humboldt
CA	**Nevada City (3,001)**	**Nevada**
CA	**San Juan Bautista (1,549)**	**San Benito**

State	Agurbs (2000 population)	County
CA	Lakeport (4,820)	Lake
CA	Red Bluff (13,147)	Tehama
CA	Ukiah (15,497)	Mendocino
CA	Yreka (7,290)	Siskiyou
ID	Bonners Ferry (2,515)	Boundary
ID	**Coeur d'Alene (34,514)**	**Kootenai**
ID	Gooding (3,384)	Gooding
ID	Horseshoe Bend (770)	Boise
ID	Jerome (7,780)	Jerome
ID	**Sun Valley (1,427)**	**Blaine**
ID	McCall (2,084)	Valley
ID	Moscow (21,291)	Latah
ID	Payette (7,054)	Payette
ID	Rexburg (17,257)	Madison
ID	**Sandpoint (6,835)**	**Bonner**
ID	Twin Falls (34,469)	Twin Falls
NV	**Carson City (52,457)**	**(Independent City)**
NV	Elko (16,708)	Elko
NV	Fallon (7,536)	Churchill
NV	Minden (2,836)	Douglas
NV	Winnemucca (7,174)	Humboldt
NV	Yerington (2,883)	Lyon
OR	Astoria (9,813)	Clatsop
OR	Baker City (9,860)	Baker
OR	**Bend (52,029)**	**Deschutes**
OR	**Grants Pass (23,003)**	**Josephine**
OR	Klamath Falls (19,462)	Klamath
OR	Lincoln City (7,437)	Lincoln
OR	Prineville (7,356)	Crook
OR	Tillamook (4,352)	Tillamook
UT	Cedar City (20,527)	Iron
UT	**Ephraim (4,505)**	**Sanpete**
UT	Heber City (7,291)	Wasatch
UT	**Logan (42,670)**	**Cache**
UT	Moab (4,779)	Grand
UT	Panguith (1,623)	Garfield
UT	**Park City (7,371)**	**Summit**
UT	**St. George (49,663)**	**Washington**

State	Agurbs (2000 population)	County
WA	Clarkston (7,337)	Asotin
WA	Colville (4,988)	Stevens
WA	Friday Harbor (1,989)	San Juan
WA	Leavenworth (2,074)	Chelan
WA	Moses Lake (14,953)	Grant
WA	Mt. Vernon (26,232)	Skagit
WA	Port Angeles (18,397)	Clallam
WA	Port Townsend (8,334)	Jefferson
WA	East Wenatchee (5,757)	Douglas

Local Flavor of Towns

Towns successfully cultivating their local flavor tend to become well-known regionally and sometimes nationally. Here are the broad categories in which a town might become known as a place to visit or relocate, along with some examples:

Tourism

Bardstown, Kentucky, which bills itself as *Where History Lives, Every Day of the Year*, has used Civil War battles, trains, bourbon distilleries and Frontier Catholicism to develop a menagerie of tourist sites. One of those sites is the birthplace of Stephen C. Foster, author of the ballad, "My Old Kentucky Home."

Ocean City, Maryland, incorporated in 1875, was a small fishing village on its way to becoming a seaside vacation destination. With 10 miles of beaches on the Atlantic Ocean, a three-mile boardwalk, and the Lifesaving Station Museum, Ocean City brings in tourists looking for a relaxing beach experience.

Other small towns that have developed thriving tourist businesses include:

- **Georgetown, South Carolina**, with its historic seaport.
- **Mountain Home, Arkansas**, which has many lakes and access to the Ozark National Forest.
- **Vero Beach, Florida**, with its location along the Treasure Coast, enhanced with 18 golf courses, and the spring training home of the Los Angeles Dodgers.
- **Cooperstown, New York**, which attracts 300,000 visitors each year to the National Baseball Hall of Fame and Museum.
- **Kitty Hawk, North Carolina**, the "birthplace of aviation" because of the Wright Brothers' first flight, and a summer resort.

Recreation

Rockport, Texas, is a recreational mecca for fishermen, birdwatchers and beachcombers. Tens of thousands of visitors are attracted to the town for the annual migration of whooping cranes and hummingbirds. It is also rapidly becoming an artists' mecca, offering amenities not often found in towns two or three times its size.

Bozeman, Montana, brings in fishermen from around the world to test their skills against the abundant populations of brown, rainbow and cutthroat trout found in the nearby Madison, Gallatin and Yellowstone streams.

Berkeley Springs, West Virginia, is well-known for its whitewater rafting on the Potomac River.

Stowe, Vermont, attracts skiers and above-timberline hikers from across the country.

St. Croix Falls, Wisconsin, offers an array of year-round outdoor recreation and events, including wilderness canoeing, camping, cross country skiing and snowmobiling.

Music and Arts

Hot Springs, Arkansas, hosts a music festival that pairs world-class musicians from major orchestras, chamber ensembles and conservatory faculties with talented pre-professional apprentices. For two weeks, playing side by side, these musicians present 23 concerts and more than 250 rehearsals open to music lovers from across the globe.

Park City, Utah, is home to the internationally renowned Sundance Film Festival.

Port Townsend, Washington, situated in the shadows of the Olympic Mountains, receives only 18 inches of rain per year. The historic seaport has long been attractive to people with artistic and creative bents and is becoming popular as a retirement town.

Among towns that feature regular outdoor park concerts are Sandpoint, Idaho; Taos, New Mexico; and Easton, Maryland. Other small towns that have strong arts and music programs include Sun Valley, Idaho; Oxford, Mississippi; Hanover, New Hampshire; Camden, Maine; Salida, Colorado; Bisbee, Arizona; the Flathead Valley, Montana; Ruidoso, New Mexico; and Natchitoches, Louisiana.

Unique Events

Telluride, Colorado, holds an annual Nothing Festival in July. It is one week of the year when nothing is scheduled to allow the locals to simply enjoy the natural pleasures of the season.

Leonardtown, Maryland, hosts the annual St. Mary's County Oyster Festival each October. The festival, which brings in more than 50,000 visitors, includes the National Oyster Shucking Championship (the winner goes to the World Event in Ireland) and the National Oyster Cook-Off.

Hollister, California, bills itself as the birthplace of the American Biker, the site of a famous incident that spawned the cult film "The Wild One." The Independence Rally, celebrating the American Biker, takes place during the first weekend in July.

Ephraim, Utah, holds a Scandinavian Festival every May to celebrate and honor the heritage of the area's early settlers. Ephraim became known as Little Denmark.

Mattoon, Illinois, the home of Lender's Bagels, bills itself as the Bagel Capital of the World. During Bagelfest in late July, the world's largest bagel breakfast is held each year (and it's free).

Three of the top 100 small towns host annual NASCAR races at tracks that bring in race fans from around the world each year. These towns and their race tracks are:

- **Long Pond, Pennsylvania** (Pocono International Raceway)
- **Talladega, Alabama** (Talladega Superspeedway)
- **Loudon, New Hampshire** (New Hampshire International Speedway)

Retirement

Petoskey, Michigan, nestled along the banks of Lake Michigan, sees its population of 7,200 surge to 25,000 during the summer as it becomes a second home for many dual-home vacationers.

Natchitoches, Louisiana, began in 1714 as a French trading post on the banks of the Red River. Its many historic homes and plantations were the setting for the movie *Steel Magnolias,* written by local author Robert Harling. Today, its relatively low cost of living, fame as a small art town and picturesque setting make it a favorite locale for retirees.

Other agurbs that are popular retiree destinations include: Camden, Maine; Marble Falls, Texas; Ruidoso, New Mexico; Prescott, Arizona; Vero Beach, Florida; and Key West, Florida.

Manufacturing

Spring Hill, Tennessee, made famous by many television commercials for Saturn Motors, is a manufacturing town with high wages and exemplary working conditions for its residents. Today, Saturn employs more than 7,000.

Keene, New Hampshire, is home to the only two domestic companies that manufacture ultraprecision machine tools. With these tools, manufacturers can create products that are within nanometers of absolute accuracy—high-tech lights in cars and homes that can outlast typical bulbs by decades, sophisticated lenses and mirrors used in products ranging from ear thermometers to laser printers and laser optics to correct severe cornea damage. One company has annual revenues of $20 million and has tripled its sales in the last three years; the other increased its revenues to $7 million in 2003. These companies, on the cusp of inventing a new industry, have the potential to transform Keene into a focal point for new technology.

Dalton, Georgia, didn't start out to be the Carpet Capital of the World. Its carpet industry began in the early 1900s when a young Dalton farm girl revived the colonial art of tufting for bedspreads. Bedspreads led to throw rugs and, in the 1950s, advances in machinery, technology and dyeing methods made the tufted carpet industry firmly entrenched in Dalton. These advances, by the way, were made by industrial entrepreneurs of Dalton.

Greencastle, Indiana, received a shock in 1986 when International Business Machines announced it was closing a local manufacturing plant. A local economic development organization was formed shortly afterward to help the town recover—and to guard against future shocks. Since 1999, Greencastle has recruited 11 new manufacturing and distribution firms, with more than $150 million invested into those new plants, other plant expansions, and new equipment.

Eagle Pass, Texas, was a sleepy border town in the early 1980s. Today, with the passage of the North American Free Trade Agreement and the subsequent growth of maquiladora plants (foreign-owned factories that assemble foreign pieces into products for export), this booming town is at the forefront of international trade. It offers employment opportunities for residents on both sides of the border.

Carson City, Nevada, is known as the "Manufacturing Hub of Nevada" because more than 150 manufacturers employ almost one in six local residents. Its close proximity to the higher-cost state of California has been a boon for Carson City.

Bowling Green, Kentucky, is home to the National Corvette Museum. Every Corvette since 1982 has been manufactured in Bowling Green.

High Tech

In today's high-tech environment it's almost essential to have a cutting-edge university nearby to better recruit high-tech companies that depend upon workforces with technical or scientific backgrounds. Here are a few of the high-tech small towns:

Rolla, Missouri, is the home of the University of Missouri at Rolla, a leading engineering school. Today the community is growing many businesses that had their beginnings in the university, such as Brewer Science, Inc., and Mosci, Inc. (both started by professors). Rolla is also able to recruit new industry because of the flow of engineering students graduating from the school.

Orrville, Ohio: Home of Smucker's

As legend has it, John Chapman—better known as Johnny Appleseed—wandered the Ohio countryside in the early 19th century, sowing apple seeds. Orrville resident Jerome Monroe Smucker first pressed cider at a mill he opened in 1897, using the apples from the trees that sprouted from Johnny Appleseed's work.

Smucker's grew from one cider press to a company with more than 2,000 employees worldwide. The J.M. Smucker Company, which manufactures fruit spreads, ice cream toppings, health and natural foods, beverages and peanut butter, has 12 manufacturing plants and distributes products in more than 70 countries.

It is still run by family members and remains headquartered in Orrville. Tim Smucker, Co-CEO with Richard Smucker, says, "We know it's important to be a good citizen, whether you're an individual or a corporation. We like to think we're a good member of the community." Smuckers has a long history of working with the town for the benefit of the local schools, library, colleges and the city itself. A history of giving back to the town has created a fruitful partnership with the community and helped make Orrville a great small town.

Blacksburg, Virginia, home of Virginia Tech, has a rich history of technological innovation. The Blacksburg Electronic Village, an outreach from Virginia Tech, serves the local community with a wide range of Internet-based services in one of the oldest such initiatives. As a result, 87 percent of its citizens are hooked into the Internet, one of the highest rates in the country.

Ames, Iowa, is home not only to Iowa State University but also to a roster of top agribusiness companies: Pioneer Hi-Bred, Monsanto, Syngenta, Cargill and others. Ames hopes to turn its Corn Belt location (Iowa is the largest producer of corn in the United States) into a global position in the burgeoning life-science industry. The agribusiness industry has invested more than $1.4 billion in new technology expansions since 1998.

Medicine

Small towns are typically not renowned for their medical facilities. However, there are several exceptions, which include:

Rochester, Minnesota, features the Mayo Clinic, one of the best-known medical clinics in the world. Due to the success of the Mayo Clinic, Rochester developed from a rural burg into a metropolitan area in its own right.

Lebanon, New Hampshire, is home to two well-known medical facilities: Dartmouth-Hitchcock Medical Center and Alice Peck Day Memorial Hospital. Dartmouth, the fourth oldest U.S. medical school, is one of the top cancer treatment and research centers in the country. The medical community in Lebanon has more than 6,000 employees in a town of only 13,000.

Columbia, Tennessee, has Maury Regional Hospital, a community-owned not-for-profit hospital. Twice the size of any other hospital between Nashville, Tennessee, and Huntsville, Alabama, the facility employs more than 2,000.

Traverse City, Michigan, counts Munson Healthcare as its largest employer and the heart of the region's medical system. With more than 350 physicians working in dozens of specialties, the hospital serves 24 counties in northern Michigan.

Bend, Oregon, has St. Charles Medical Center, a regional hospital covering the largest medical service district in the state. It is nationally known for its orthopedic, cardiac and obstetrical services.

Yankton, South Dakota, is blessed with both the Avera Sacred Heart Hospital and South Dakota Human Services Center—Mickelson Center for Neurosciences, which cover a multi-state area. These two institutions employ more than 1,500 people.

Education

Probably the biggest surprise in researching the top small towns in the United States was how few of them had a four-year college. Of the top 100 agurbs, only 16 had a four-year college. They are:

- Ames, Iowa (Iowa State University)
- Beaufort, South Carolina (University of South Carolina—Beaufort)
- Bowling Green, Kentucky (Western Kentucky University)
- Bozeman, Montana (Montana State University)
- Cape Girardeau, Missouri (Southeast Missouri State University)
- Durango, Colorado (Fort Lewis College)
- East Stroudsburg, Pennsylvania (East Stroudsburg University)
- Greencastle, Indiana (DePauw University)
- Hanover, New Hampshire (Dartmouth College)
- Harrisonburg, Virginia (Eastern Mennonite University and James Madison University)
- Kearney, Nebraska (University of Nebraska—Kearney)
- Logan, Utah (Utah State University)
- Natchitoches, Louisiana (Northwestern State University)
- Oxford, Mississippi (University of Mississippi)
- Sierra Vista, Arizona (University of Arizona South)
- Whitewater, Wisconsin (University of Wisconsin—Whitewater)

Of the other 297 agurbs, 66 have four-year colleges or universities. Of these 66 agurbs, 14 have two or more colleges or universities:

- Aberdeen, South Dakota
- Arkadelphia, Arkansas
- Bemidji, Minnesota
- Brattleboro, Vermont
- Cleveland, Tennessee
- Ithaca, New York
- Keene, New Hampshire
- Montpelier, Vermont
- Moscow, Idaho
- Oneonta, New York
- Orangeburg, South Carolina
- Quincy, Illinois
- Waterville, Maine
- Winona, Minnesota

Index

Abbeville, SC, 152
ABC Bancorp, 96
Aberdeen, SD, 156, 167
Abilene, KS, 62, 156
Adelphia Communications Corporation, 114
Agracel, Inc., x–xi
Agurban migration/Third Wave, xiii, 137–38
Agurbs:
  cost of doing business, 19
  definition, xiii
  employment, 57, 131–32, 134, 136
  future, 137-41
  growth comparisons, 9, 131, 134, 136, 138
  housing, 138
  income, 9, 131, 132–33, 134, 136
  population, 9-10, 134, 136
  winners, by region, 149–60
Ahmeek, MI, 153
Airplane technology, 19
Alabama Power, New Industries Division, 98
Albany, KY, 153
Alcoa, 105
Alexandria, MN, 154
Alice Peck Day Memorial Hospital, 166
"All Natural" Theme Park of America
  (see Mackinac Island, Michigan)
Allen, Dr. John C., 18
Alley, Kirstie, 135
Alma, KS, 156
Amana Colonies, IA, 68
Amelia Island Plantation, 59
Ameritech, 44
Ames, IA, 133, 146, 152, 166–67
Apalachicola, FL, 58, 146, 150
Appleseed, Johnny, 165
Arbor Vitae, WI, 155
Area Development Online, 18
Arkadelphia, AR, 157, 167
Armstrong, Lance, 26
Astoria Mill, 97
Astoria, OR, 97, 159

Augusta, ME, 135
Auto Research Center, 111
Avera Sacred Heart Hospital, 166
AviaCode, 78
Badger Army Ammunition Plant, 116
Bagel Capital of the World (see Mattoon, IL)
Baker, Don, 34
Baker City, OR, 159
Bank of Astoria, 97
Baraboo, WI, 116, 147, 155
Bardstown, KY, 146, 153, 161
Barnes, Linda, 67
Barrett, John, 113
Bartlesville, OK, 14
Basinger, Kim, 44
Bastian, Lisa A., 18
Bauer, Bill, 27–28
Beal, Dave, 57
L.L. Bean, 19
Beaver Dam, WI, 155
Beaufort, SC, 64, 167
Beautiful Mind, A, 3
C.H. Becksvoort, 63
Belfast, ME, 149
Belvidere, IL, 79
Bemidji, MN, 154, 167
Bend, OR, 119, 133, 148, 159, 166
Benoit, Paul, 97
Benthin, Dorrene, 13
Benton County, AR, 117
Bentonville, AR, 23, 117
Berkeley Springs, WV, 145, 150, 162
Berlin, OH, 63
Bethlehem Steel, 17
Big Rapids, MI, 154
Bigfork, ME, 64
Bisbee, AZ, 106, 162
Bittersweet: The Story of the Heath Candy Co.
  (Heath), 87
Blacksburg Electronic Village, The, 166
Blacksburg, VA, 149, 166

Blaine County, ID, 108
Blairsville, GA, 150
Blattner, Tim, 129
Blue Crab Festival, 45
Blue Hill, ME, 64, 145, 149
Blue Ridge, GA, 150
Bonners Ferry, ID, 159
Boone, NC, 107, 151
Boonyack Comeback, The, 13
Bowling Green, KY, 133, 146, 153, 165, 167
Bowling Green, OH, 135
Bozeman, MT, 133, 147, 156, 162, 167
Bradshaw, Terry, 8
"Brain Bank":
  building, 65–68
  defined, 64–65
Brainerd, MN, 154
Branding:
  defined, 101
  development, 102–04
  growing, 105–06
Branson, MO, 2, 42–43, 102, 147, 154
Braselton, GA, 44
Brattleboro, VT, 150, 167
Breckenridge, CO, 155
Brevard, NC, 107, 151
Brewer Science, Inc., 165
Brewton, AL, 150
"Bricks to Chips" (see Danville, IL)
Bridgeville, CA
Broadband, 13
Brokaw, Tom, 135
Bronson, FL, 150
Brookings, SD, 156
Brookville, IN, 153
Brunswick, GA, 68, 133,146, 150
Buena Vista, CO, 7, 135, 147, 156
Buffalo, WY, 156
Buffalo County, NE, 75
Bunge Foods, xi
Bureau of Community Development
  (University of Washington), 27
Bush, George, 62
Cabela, Dick, 85

Cabela, Mary, 85
Cabela's, Inc., 85
Cable News Network, 66
Cadillac, MI, 154
Cairo, IL, 121
Calamity Jane, 129
Caledonia, OH, 62
Calhoun, GA, 11, 150
Camden, ME, 135, 145, 149, 162, 164
Camdenton, MO, 59, 147, 154
"Can Do Poem, The," 28
Can-Do attitude, characteristics, 25–30, 35
Cape Girardeau, MO, 119–30, 133, 135,
147, 154, 167
  case study, 119–30
  demographics, 119, 121
  history, 120
  survey, 127
Carder, Norma, 65
Cargill, 166
"Carpet Capital of the World" (see Dalton, GA)
Carson, Johnny, 33
Carson City, NV, 133, 135, 148, 159, 165
Carter, Jimmy, 62
Carteret County (NC) Economic
  Development Council, 49
Cashmere, WA, 43
Caterpillar, 45
Cedar City, UT, 159
Celina, OH, 155
Central City, CO, 155
Chapman, John (see Appleseed, Johnny)
Chappell, NE, 85
Charles City, IA, 113
Charlevoix, MI, 154
Cheraw, SC, 152
Chestertown, MD, 149
Chicago Bulls, 72-73
Chickasaw Bluffs, MS, 64
Chikamin Hotel (see Hotel Edelweiss)
Chillicothe, OH, 155
Chilton County (AL) Chamber of
  Commerce Leadership Course, 80
Chipley, FL, 150

Christmas Lake Village, 83
"Church in the Wildwood, The," 112
City of Roses on the River (*see* Cape
    Girardeau, MO)
Clanton, AL, 80, 146, 150
Clarkston, WA, 59, 148, 160
Clarksville, AR, 157
Clemens, Samuel (*see* Twain, Mark)
Cleveland, TN, 152, 167
Clewiston, FL, 150
Clinton, AR, 157
Clinton, Bill, 62
Clintonville, WI, 77–78, 147, 155
Coca-Cola, xi
Cocker, Joe, 135
Cody, WY, 156
Coeur d'Alene, ID, 73, 133, 148, 159
Coil Craft, 36
Coldwater, MI, 154
Collins, MS, 151
Columbia, TN, 64, 119, 135, 166
Columbus, IN, 11, 41–42, 119, 133, 146, 153
Columbus, MT, 156
Columbus, NC, 107, 151
Colusa, CA, 158
Colville, WA, 80, 148, 160
Comer, Gary, 7
Common Pleas Courthouse, 121
Communities:
    banks, statistics, 95
    characteristics, 1, 7
    personality types, 30–32, 34
    Eagles, 32
    Jackals, 31–32
    Moles, 31
    Mules, 30-31
    resources and strengths, 56–68
    service costs study, 86
    vision, 41–48
    Web sites, 108
Community Development Foundation
    (MS), 71
ConAgra, 72
Concord, NH, 133, 135, 145, 149

ConocoPhillips, 14
Consolidated Communications, 93
Cookeville, TN, 152
Coolidge, Calvin, 62
Cooper Tire & Rubber, 11
Cooperstown, NY, 149, 161
Corning, NY, 11, 58, 149
Corsica, OH, 62
Corsicana, TX, 51, 158
Cortez, CO, 155
Coudersport, PA, 114
*Country Bound: Trade Your Business Suit
    Blues for Blue Jean Dreams* (Ross and
    Ross), 7
Crawford, CO, 135
CREATE, 71
Creede, CO, 155
Crested Butte, CO, 155
Crockett, Davy, 62
Crossroads of Opportunity
    (*see* Effingham, IL)
Crossville, TN, 61, 146, 152
CSX Rail, 95
Cullman, AL, 150
Cummins Inc., 11, 41
Cummins Foundation, The, 41
Daily Astorian, The, 97
Dakota Foundation, The, 66
Dalton, GA, 64, 150, 164
Danville, IL, 105, 153
Dartmouth College, 167
Dartmouth-Hitchcock Medical Center, 166
W.B. Davis Hosiery Mill, 47
Dawsonville, GA, 59, 146, 151
Death Tax Newsletter, 98
Decatur Daily (AL), 98–99
Decatur, AL, 98
Decatur, IL, 105
Decatur, TX, 46, 148, 158
Deer Isle, ME, 64
De Funiak Springs, FL, 150
Delta, CO, 155
Dement, Margaret Randol, 129
Denison, TX, 62

Density/acres per person, 21
Dent, Harry S., 13
DePauw University, 167
Deregulation (see Staggers Act)
Dillingham, AK, 158
Dixon, IL, 62
Dodge Center, MN, 154
Dodge City, KS, 156
Dodgeville, WI, 7, 119, 147, 155
Door County, WI, 68
Double Springs, AL, 98, 150
Douglas, GA, 33, 146, 151
Dreamtowns.com, 9
Duni Plastics, 15
Dunn, NC, 151
Durango, CO, 89, 132, 147, 155, 167
Durant, OK, 51, 115, 133, 135, 148, 158
Durham, Annelle, 8
Eagar, AZ, 157
Eagle Pass, TX, 133, 148, 158, 164
E. Stroudsburg, PA, 145, 149, 167
East Stroudsburg University, 167
East Wenatchee, WA, 160
Eastern Mennonite University, 167
Easton, MD, 64, 133, 145, 149, 162
Eatonton, GA, 151
Eddens, Quince, 98
Edenton, NC, 151
Edison, Thomas, 89
Effingham, IL, x–xii, 42, 48, 66, 86, 95, 153
    Crossroads of Opportunity, x
    economic crisis, x
    economic renewal, xi
Eisenhower, Dwight D., 62
Eliot, T.S., 129
Elizabeth, CO, 155
Elizabethtown, KY, 153
Elizabethtown, NC, 151
Elk Point, SD, 156
Elko, NV, 159
Employment, statistics, 57, 112, 117, 136
"Energy Capital of the Nation"
    (see Gillette, WY)
Energy Park, 33

Enterprise Zones (E/Z), 86
Entrepreneurs:
    characteristics, 84–92
    defined, 84
Ephraim, UT, 148, 159, 163
Escapule, Dusty, 40
Espanola, NM, 157
Estancia, NM, 157
Eufaula, AL, 77, 146, 150
Eufaula National Wildlife Refuge, 77
"Eufaula 2020" Strategic Plan, 77
Eureka, CA, 158
Fairview, TN, 152
Fallon, NV, 159
Farm Progress Show, 68
Farmer City, IL, 16
Farmington, MO, 154
Farmington, NM, 157
Farmland National Beef, 96
Faulkner and Yoknapatawpha Conference, 43
Fergus Falls, MN, 154
Fiberteq, LLC, 105
Findlay, OH, 11, 155
First Bank and Trust, 99
Flathead Valley Area, MT, 64, 162
Flower Industries, 45
Fond du Lac, WI, 155
Forbes, 13
Forest, MS, 151
Forrester, Stephen, 97
Fort Lewis College, 167
Fort Payne, AL, 47, 98, 132, 146, 150
Foster, Stephen C., 161
Fraser, Charles, 58–59
French Lick, IN, 44
Friday Harbor, WA, 148, 160
Gainesville, GA, 151
Galena, IL, 153
Galesburg, IL, 61, 80, 135, 153
Gallup, NM, 157
Garden City, KS, 72, 133, 147, 156
Garden Jubilee, 46
Gaylord, MI, 154
Georgetown, SC, 133, 146, 152, 161

Gershenson, David, 8
Gilder, George, 113
Gillette, WY, 33, 119, 133, 147, 157
Gimre's Shoes, 97
Girardot, Jean Baptiste, 122
Glasgow, KY, 153
Glenwood Springs, CO, 21, 132, 147, 156
Globalization, 17
Globe, AZ, 157
Goals, setting and achieving, 49–53
Golden Eagles Top 100 Agurbs:
    characteristics, 145
    listing, by region, 145-48
    methodology, 144-45
    selection criteria, 143-45
Golf Capital of Tennessee (see Crossville, TN)
Gooding, ID, 159
Grand Island, NE, 156
Grand Marsais, MN, 154
Grand Teton National Park, 55
Grants, NM, 157
Grants Pass, OR, 59, 133, 135, 148, 159
Grantsburg, WI, 155
Grass Valley, CA, 51
Great Northern Railway Company, 26
Greilickville, MI, 154
Greencastle, IN, 146, 153, 164, 167
Greensboro, AL, 150
Greensburg, IN, 153
Greenville, TN, 62, 133, 146, 152
Griffith, Andy, 8
Guymon Pioneer Days Rodeo, 115
Guymon, OK, 115, 148, 158
GVNW Consulting, 13
Hamilton, MT, 156
Hammond, LA, 80, 108, 133, 147, 157
"HandMade in America" Initiative
    (see Western North Carolina)
Hannibal, MO, 61–62, 135, 154
Hanover, NH, 162, 167
Hansen, Chris, 11–12
Harding, Warren G., 62
Hardy County, WV, 108
Harling, Robert, 163

Harrison, AR, 157
Harrisonburg, VA, 145, 149, 167
Hastings, MI, 80, 146, 154
Hawarden, IA, 35–36, 152
Hayseedville, 2
Hayward, WI, 155
Heath, Dick, 87
Heath Brothers Confectionary, 87
Heber City, UT, 159
Helena, MT, 135, 156
Hendersonville Apple Festival, 46
Hendersonville, NC, 46, 50, 61, 133, 146, 151
Hickson, W.E., 89
Highland, IL, 103
Highlands, NC, 107, 146, 151
Hillsboro, TX, 61, 148, 158
Hilton Head Island, SC, 58–59, 133,
    146, 152
Hines, Duncan, 135
Hinesville, GA, 151
Holaday, Bart, 66
Holiday World, 83–84
Hollister, CA, 51, 163
Holmes, P.K., 117
Holmes County, OH, 55
Home Baking, 97
Hoosier Southern Railroad, 29
Hoosiers, 74
Hoover, Herbert, 62
Hope, AR, 62
Horberg, Paul, 11
Horseshoe Bend, ID, 159
Hotel Edelweiss, 27
Hot Springs, AR, 44, 62, 132, 147, 157, 162
Hot Sulphur Springs, CO, 156
Howorth, Richard, 43
Hueber, Betsy, 14
Hunnicutt, Jack, 96
Huntsville, AL, 98
Hustead, Dorothy, 47
Hutchinson, MN, 154
Hyde Park, NY, 62
IBM (International Business Machines),
    11, 164

IKO Industries, 105
Illinois Central (IC), 95
Illinois Chamber of Commerce, 57
Illinois Valley Area Chamber of
    Commerce and Economic Development, 34
Income, statistics, 9, 57, 119, 131–34, 136
Independence Rally (*see* Hollister, CA)
International Economic Development
    Council (IEDC), 115
International Telework Association and
    Council, 12
Internet use, 19–20
logistics, Inc., 19
Iowa, state of, 65
Iowa City, IA, 106
Iowa State University, 166, 167
Ithaca, NY, 149, 167
Jackson, David E., 55
Jackson, GA, 151
Jackson, MO, 120, 122
Jackson, Phil, 72–73
Jackson, WY, 55, 147, 157
Jackson County, IN, 22
Jackson Hole, WY (*see* Jackson, WY)
James, Frank, 129
James, Jesse, 129
James Madison University, 167
Jasper, IN, 153
Jasper, TX, 158
Jaxon Jr., Jay, 77
Jay, OK, 158
Jefferson, GA, 150
Jefferson City, MO, 135, 154
Jekyll Island, GA, 68
Jenison, Ed, 99
Jenison, Kevin, 99
Jenison, Ned, 99
Jerome, ID, 159
Jobs Plus Economic Development Group
    (ID), 73
Johnson, Andrew, 62
Johnson, Lyndon B., 62
Johnson, Tom, 98
Johnson City, TX, 62

Jones, James, 135
Joplin, Scott, 135
Jordan, Michael, 72
Juneau, AK, 135, 158
Kalispell, MT, 64, 147, 156
Karlgaard, Rich, 13
Kearney, NE, 75, 85, 119, 133, 147, 155, 167
Keillor, Garrison, 4
Keene, NH, 149, 164, 167
Kendallville, IN, 153
Kennedy, Robert F., 25
Kerrville, TX, 51, 158
Key West, FL, 150, 164
Kiawah Island Resort, 59
Kimberling City, MO, 154
King, Jr., Martin Luther, 81
Kirkman, Don, 49
Kitty Hawk, NC, 151, 161
Klamath Falls, OR, 159
Kmart, 23
Knox County (IL) Teen Court, 80
Knudtson, Jay, 125–26
Knutsen Insurance, 97
Koch, Barb, 34
Koch, Bill, 83
Koch, Louis, 83–84
Koch, Will, 84
Kosciusko, MS, 135, 151
Kramer, Tommy, 115–16
S.S. Kresge (*see* Kmart)
Krispy Kreme, xi, 95
La Follette, TN, 152
Lagrange, IN, 153
Lake City, FL, 150
Lake Placid, NY, 59, 149
Lakeport, CA, 159
Lamar, MO, 62
Lancaster, KY, 153
"Land for the Adventurous, A"
    (*see* Hardy County, WV)
Lander, WY, 157
Lands' End, 7, 19
Las Vegas, NM, 157
LaSalle, IL, 34

Lavonia, GA, 151
Leadership:
    characteristics, 73–81
    defined, 69–70
Leadership and Spirit (Moxley), 69
Leadership Barry County (MI), 80–81
Leadership Garden City (KS), 72
Leaf, Inc., 87
Leavenworth, WA, 26–28, 30, 43, 102,
    107, 160
Lebanon, KY, 153
Lebanon, MO, 154
Lebanon, NH, 133, 145, 149, 166
Lender's Bagels, 163
Leonardtown, MD, 149, 163
Levering, Frank, 8
Lewis and Clark Expedition, 120
Lewisburg, PA, 149
Lexington, TN, 152
Liberal, KS, 62, 147, 156
Lieb, Bobby, 89
Life on the Mississippi (Twain), 124
Lifelong Learning Center (*see* Norfolk, NE)
Lifesaving Station Museum, 161
Limbaugh, Rush, 129, 135
Lincoln City, OR, 159
Litehouse Dressings, 63
Little Brown Church in the Vale, 112
Little Denmark (*see* Ephraim, UT)
Little St. Simons Island, GA, 68
Livingston, MT, 156
Llano, TX, 158
Local Flavor, defined, 63–64, 161–66
Logan, UT, 59, 133, 148, 159, 167
Long Pond, PA, 163
Loudon, NH, 163
Lowe's, 11
Lucedale, MS, 151
Ludington, MI, 154
Lumpkin School of Business, 93
Lumpkin, Iverson A., 93
Lumpkin, Richard A. (Dick), 93–94
Lynchburg, TN, 152
Mackinac Island, MI, 101–02, 135, 146, 154

Madill, OK, 158
Main Line Pictures, 44
Main Street, 51
Manassas, VA, 63
Manufacturing, statistics, 57
Manufacturing Hub of Nevada
    (*see* Carson City, NV)
*Manufacturing Works: The Vital Link
    Between Production and Prosperity*
    (Zimmerman and Beal), 57
Marble Falls, TX, 148, 158, 164
Marengo, IA, 152
Marion, IL, 33, 146, 153
Mason City, IA, 152
MASS MoCA (Museum of Contemporary
    Art), 113
Mattoon, IL, 66, 93, 153, 163
Maury Alliance, The, 64
Maury Regional Hospital, 166
Mayo Clinic, 166
Maytag, 11
McCall, ID, 159
McEntire, Reba, 135
McLean, George, 71
McLeodUSA, 93
McPherson, KS, 156
Mellencamp, John, 135
Mena, AR, 157
Menomonie, WI, 51, 155
Metropolitan Statistical Area (MSA):
    counties, 2–3, 131–32
    defined, xiii, 2, 46, 143–44
Mid America Designs, 42
Middlebury, VT, 150
Middletown, VA, 149
Milan, IN, 74
Milken Institute, 134, 136
Miller, J. Irwin, 41
Millersburg, OH, 147, 155
Milton, MA, 62
Minden, NV, 159
Minot, ND, 156
Miracle Town (Price), 27
Mississippi River, 74, 120, 125

Moab, UT, 159
Mohawk Industries, 11
Monarch Butterfly Festival, 45–46
Monett, MO, 154
Monsanto, 166
Montana State University, 167
Monticello, GA, 151
Montpelier, VT, 135, 150, 167
Montrose, CO, 156
Moore Haven, FL, 150
Moorefield, WV, 145, 150
Mooresville, NC, 111–12, 151
Morehead City, NC, 49, 119, 146, 151
Morgantown, WV, 51, 150
Mosci, Inc., 165
Moscow, ID, 159
Moses Lake, WA, 74, 119, 148, 160
Moultrie, GA, 96, 151
Mount Airy, NC, 8
Mount Ida, AR, 157
Mount Pleasant, MI, 154
Mt. Pleasant, TX, 51, 158
Mount St. Helens, 74
Mt. Vernon, IL, 153, 160
Mountain Home, AR, 147, 157, 161
Mountain View, AR, 157
*Moving to a Small Town: A Guidebook
    for Moving from Urban to Rural America*
    (Urbanska and Levering), 8
Moxley, Russ S., 69
Munson Healthcare, 166
Murfreesboro, AR, 157
Murphy, NC, 107, 151
"Music on Main," 46
Nahunta, GA, 151
NASCAR, 111, 163
Nash, John, 3, 5
Nash Equilibrium Theory, 4, 68
Nashua, IA, 112
Nashville, IN, 153
Natchitoches, LA, 119, 147, 157, 162–63, 167
National Baseball Hall of Fame, 161
National Corvette Museum, 165
National Tom Sawyer Days, 61

Nauvoo, IL, 153
Nevada City, CA, 22, 135, 148, 158
Nevada County, CA, 108
New Bern, NC, 152
New Gloucester, ME, 63, 149
New Hampshire International Speedway, 163
New Iberia, LA, 157
Newberry, OR, 62
Newberry, SC, 33, 119, 146, 152
Newport, AR, 117
Newport, TN, 59, 152
Newspapers, statistics, 98
Newton, IA, 11, 152
No-Name Mountain, 60
Norfolk Southern
    (*see* Hoosier Southern Railroad)
Norfolk, NE, 33, 156
North Adams, MA, 113, 149
North American Free Trade Agreement
    (NAFTA), 164
North Carolina Speedway, 112
North Pole, AK, 158
North Vernon, IN, 153
Northern Alabama Industrial
    Development Association, 98
Northwestern State University, 167
Nothing Festival, 163
Oak Hill, WV, 150
Oakdale, LA, 157
Ocean City, MD, 145, 149, 161
Office of Management and Budget
    (OMB), 144
Oinky's Ribs, 63
Okeechobee, FL, 150
Oneonta, NY, 167
Oppedahl, Carl, 48
Orangeburg, SC, 152, 167
Orchard Gap, NC, 8
Oregon Department of Environmental
    Quality (ODEQ), 97
Original Winter Resort of the South
    (*see* Thomasville, GA)
Orrville, OH, 135, 155, 165
Osceola, IA, 152

Owen, Jim, 2
Owens-Corning, 105
Oxford Conference for the Book, 43
Oxford, MS, 43, 119, 146, 151, 162, 167
Oxford, NC, 152
Pagosa Springs, CO, 156
Paige, Satchel, 32
Palmas del Mar Resort, 59
Panacea, FL, 46
Panguith, UT, 159
Paragould, AR, 63, 132, 147, 157
Paris, IL, 99, 116, 153
Paris, TN, 152
Paris Beacon Publishing Company, 99
Paris Beacon-News, 99
Park City, UT, 64, 133, 148, 159, 162
Park Rapids, MN, 154
Paw-to-Paw Competition, 55
Payette, ID, 159
Pella, IA, 153
PEOPLE approach, 36–40, 85
    Plan, 36–37
    Enlist allies, 36–37
    Observe opponents, 36–38
    Present the plan, 36, 38
    Lead by example, 36, 39
    Engage others, 36, 39–40
Pepsi, xi
Peru, IL, 153
Peterson, LaVerne, 27
Petoskey, MI, 133, 146, 154, 163
"Peyton Place" factor, 139
Philadelphia, MS, 83, 146, 151
Phillips Petroleum Company
    (see ConocoPhillips)
Picayune, MS, 52, 146, 151
Pierre, SD, 135, 156
Pine City, MN, 154
Pinehurst, NC, 152
Pioneer Hi-Bred, 166
Pippen, Scottie, 72
Plains, GA, 62
Plaquemine, LA, 157
Pleasanton, TX, 158

Pocono International Raceway, 163
Polk, James K., 135
Ponchatoula, LA, 49
Pontotoc, MS, 151
Population, statistics, 9, 62, 112, 117, 119,
    121, 131, 134, 136, 144, 145–60
Port Angeles, WA, 160
Port Townsend, WA, 133, 148, 160, 162
Potter, Bob, 73–74
Prescott, AZ, 59, 108, 132, 147, 157, 164
Presley, Elvis, 62, 135
Price, Ted, 27
Princeton, IN, 153
Prineville, OR, 159
Proactive Approach, defined, 91
Pryor, NM, 158
Pulaski, TN, 152
Quad-Graphics, 15
Quincy, IL, 153, 167
Reagan, Ronald, 62
Red Bluff, CA, 159
Red Lodge, MT, 156
Red Wing, MN, 154
"Relaxing in Wisconsin's Back Yard"
    (see Whitewater, WI)
Rexburg, ID, 159
Rhinelander, WI, 155
Ridgeland, SC, 152
Rigas family, 114
River Campus (Southeast Missouri State
    University School of Visual and
    Performing Arts), 124, 130
River Heritage Mural Association (MO), 129
Roaring 2000s, The (Dent), 13
Roberson, Roger, 16
Robinson, IL, 65, 87, 135, 153
Rochester, MN, 166
Rockefeller, John D., 55
Rockingham, NC, 112
Rockport, TX, 148, 158, 162
Rocky Mount, VA, 51, 145, 149
Rogers, AR, 23
Rogers, Will, 12
Rolla, MO, 154, 165

Rolla, ND, 156
Roosevelt, Franklin D., 62
Ross, Marilyn, 7
Ross, Tom, 7
Ruby Ranch, CO, 48
Ruidoso, NM, 148, 162, 158, 164
Rumford, ME, 149
Russellville, AL, 98, 150
Russellville, AR, 157
Rust, Gary, 128
Rust, Jon, 128–29
Rust, Rex, 128
Rust Communications, 128–29
Rutledge, TN, 152
Saarinen, Eliel, 41
Sacred Hoops (Jackson), 72–73
Sailor Springs, IL, 44
St. Charles Medical Center, 166
St. Croix Falls, WI, 147, 162, 155
Ste. Genevieve, MO, 155
St. George, UT, 108, 133, 148, 159
St. Marks, FL, 46
St. Mary's, GA, 151
St. Mary's County Oyster Festival, 163
St. Simons Island, GA, 68
St. Vincent's Seminary, 124
Salida, CO, 162
Salina, KS, 156
Salisbury, MD, 149
Samuel, David, 66
Samuel L. Clemens Arts & Crafts Festival, 61
San Juan Bautista, CA, 148, 158
San Juan Islands, WA, 68
Sandburg, Carl, 41, 61, 135
Sandpoint, ID, 59, 63, 148, 162
Sanford, ME, 46, 145, 149
Sanford, NC, 152
Santa Claus Land (*see* Holiday World)
Santa Claus, IN, 83, 135, 153
Saturn Motors, 164
Sauk County (WI) Economic
    Development Corporation, 116
Sault Ste. Marie, MI 154
SBA (*see* US Small Business Administration)

Scandinavian Festival, 163
Schneider Logistics, 66
Scivally, Dennis, 120
Scott City, MO, 125
Scottsboro, AL, 98, 150
Sea Island, GA, 68
Sea Pines Plantation, 58
Seagrave Fire Apparatus Plant, 78
Searcy, AR, 157
Sedalia, MO, 135, 154
Seibert, Pete, 60
Semo Port, 125–26
Senge, Peter, 69
September 11, 2001, 22, 25, 77
7½ Keys to Small-Town Success, 22
    Key #1—Adopt a Can-Do Attitude, 25–40
    Key #2—Shape Your Vision, 41–54
    Key #3—Leverage Your Resources, 55–68
    Key #4—Raise Up Strong Leaders, 69–81
    Key #5—Encourage an Entrepreneurial
        Spirit, 83–92
    Key #6—Maintain Local Control, 93–100
    Key #7—Build Your Brand, 101–09
    Key #7½—Embrace the Teeter-Totter
        Factor, 111–18
Seymour, IN, 135, 153
Shedd, Randall, 18
Shell Lake, WI, 155
Shelton Sr., Barrett C., 98
Shepherd, TX, 158
Sheridan, WY, 156
Shorebank Enterprises, 97
Show Me Center, 122–24
Sidewalk Chalk Art Show, 46
Sidney, NE, 85, 156
Sierra Vista, AZ, 106, 167
Silver City, NM, 8, 158
*Simple Living: One Couple's Search for a
    Better Life* (Urbanska and Levering), 8
Small towns, growth trends, 15–22
Smith, Larry, 66
Smucker, Jerome Monroe, 165
Smucker, Richard, 165
Smucker, Tim, 165

J.M. Smucker Company, 165
Snow King, 55
Snowflake, AZ, 157
Snyder's Mill, MS, 64
Sock Capital of the World (see Fort Payne, AL)
Sopchoppy, FL, 46, 146, 150
South Dakota Human Services Center-
    Mickelson Center for Neurosciences, 166
Southeast Missouri Regional Port
    Authority (see Semo Port)
Southeast Missouri State University, 120–21,
    122, 124, 127, 128, 167
Southwest Airlines, 17
Spinner.com, 66
Spirit Lake, IA, 153
Sprague Electric, 113
Spring Hill, TN, 135, 146, 152, 164
Square Books, 43
Stafford, Saralyn, 33
Staggers Act, 16
Starkville, MS, 151
State Universities Retirement System of
    Illinois, 11
Statesboro, GA, 151
Statesville, NC, 51
Staunton, VA, 62
Steamboat Springs, CO, 156
Steel Magnolias, 163
Stephenville, TX, 158
Stevens Point, WI, 155
Stillwater, OK, 51, 158
Stilwell, OK, 158
Stonewall, TX, 62
Storm King Trail Memorial
    (see Glenwood Springs, CO)
Stowe, VT, 145, 150, 162
Sturgeon Bay, WI, 155
Sturgis, SD, 156
Sullivan, Dave, 99
Sun Valley, ID, 148, 159–62
Sundance Film Festival, 162
Sur, Larry, 66
Sweetwater, TN, 152
Sylva, NC, 107, 152

Syngenta, 166
Systrand Presta Engines Systems, 105
Talladega Superspeedway, 163
Talladega, AL, 150, 163
Tamberrino, Frank, 64
Tampico, IL, 62
Taos, NM, 133, 148, 158, 162
Tax Increment Financing (TIF), 33, 86
Tazewell, TN, 152
Tech poles, 134–35
Teeter-Totter Factor:
    defined, 11
    lessons, 113–16
Telecommuting/teleworking, 11–12
Telecosm (Gilder), 113
Tell City, IN, 29, 94–95, 153
Tell City Chair Company, 29
Telluride, CO, 147, 156, 163
Ten Mile Garden, 120
Teton Village, 55
Thatcher, AZ, 157
Third Wave, xiii, 10, 137–38, 139, 140
Thomaston, GA, 14–15, 45, 151
Thomaston Mills, 14
Thomaston-Upson (GA) Chamber of
    Commerce, 14
Thomasville, GA, 51, 133, 146, 151
Tillamook, OR, 159
TNS Mills, Inc., 112
Tombstone, AZ, 40, 102, 147, 157
"Town Too Tough to Die" (see
    Tombstone, AZ)
Townsend, MT, 156
Trail of Tears State Park, 121
Transportation, 16–17, 19, 67, 95
Traverse City, MI, 133, 146, 154, 166
Trek Bicycle Corporation, 26
Trendbending Initiative, 75
Tripod, 113
Truck City (see Clintonville, WI)
Truman, Harry S, 62, 129
Truth or Consequences, NM, 158
Tualitin, OR, 13
Tupelo, MS, 62, 71, 135, 151

Tuscola, IL, 153
Twain, Mark, 61, 124, 129, 135
Twin Falls, ID, 159
Ukiah, CA, 159
US Small Business Administration (SBA), 97
University of Arizona South, 167
University of Iowa, 106
University of Mississippi, 167
University of Missouri at Rolla, 165
University of Nebraska-Kearney, 167
University of Nebraska-Lincoln, 18
University of South Carolina-Beaufort, 167
University of Wisconsin-Whitewater, 167
Upper Lake, CA, 8
Urbanska, Wanda, 8
Utah, state of, 78
Utah State University, 167
Utz, Bob, 48
Uvalde, TX, 158
Vail, CO, 60, 132, 147, 156
Van Wert, OH, 155
Vero Beach, FL, 133, 146, 150, 161, 164
Vesta Junior Women's Club, 27
Vicksburg, MS, 151
Vilsack, Tom, 65
Virginia Tech, 166
Vision 2020 Strategic Plan, 124–25
Wakulla Springs State Park, 45
Walker, MN, 154
Wall Drug Store, 47
Wall, SD, 47
Wall Street Journal, The, 103
Wal-Mart, 18, 23, 33, 117
Walton, Sam, 18, 23, 117
Ware, Ross, 45
Warsaw, IN, 153
Waterloo, WI, 26, 155
Watertown, SD, 156
Waterville, ME, 66, 149, 167
Wathen, Greg, 29
Waverly, OH, 33, 147, 155
Weber State University, 78
Wellsboro, PA, 149
West Branch, IA, 62

West Branch, MI, 67, 154
West Plains, MO, 155
Western Kentucky University, 167
Western North Carolina, 107
"Where History Lives, Every Day of the Year"
    (see Bardstown, KY)
White River Junction, VT, 150
Whitefish, MT, 64
Whitewater, WI, 108, 147, 155, 167
Wi-Fi, 13
Wilkesboro, NC, 10, 152
Williams, Tennessee, 129
Williams, Thurston, 8
Wilmington, OH, 155
Wilson, NC, 152
Wilson, Woodrow, 62
Winfrey, Oprah, 135
Winnemucca, NV, 159
Winona, MN, 154, 167
Winterset, IA, 153
Wiscasset, ME, 149
Wizard of Oz House, 62
Wooster, OH, 51
Work ethic, 18-19
Wright Brothers, 161
Wyman, Jerri, 127–28
Wyman, John, 127–28
Yager, Mike, 42
Yamaha Music, 15
Yankton, SD, 135, 156, 166
Yates Company, 83
Yerington, NV, 159
Yreka, CA, 159
Zimmerman, Fred, 57

Bibliography

Chapter One

Keillor, Garrison. *A Prairie Home Companion.*

Rueter, Frank. *In the Heart of Ozark Mountain Country.* Reed Spring: White Oak Press, 1992.

Chapter Two

Bastian, Lisa A. "Companies Rediscover Down-Home Advantages," *Area Development* (April 1999): 52–59.

Bastian, "Putting Rural on the Map," *Area Development* (December 2002): 23–25.

Burkhardt, Larry. Survey by author, Effingham, IL, 2002.

Comer, Gary. As quoted on www.landsend.com. © 2003, Lands' End, Inc. Used with permission.

Dent, Harry S., Jr. *The Roaring 2000s: Building the Wealth and Lifestyle You Desire in the Greatest Boom in History.* New York: Touchstone, 2002.

Erskine, Dwight. Interview by Lisa Huston, Effingham, IL, 21 November 2003.

Fallows, James. *Free Flight: From Airline Hell to a New Age of Travel.* Cambridge: Perseua Books Group, 2001.

"Fortune 500 Largest US Corporations," *FORTUNE* (14 April 2003).

Gershenson, David. As quoted on www.silvercity-business.com.

Hansen, Chris. Telephone interview by author, Effingham, IL, 8 January 2003.

Hartill, Lane. "From City to Soil," *The Christian Science Monitor Online* (7 November 2001). © 2001, *The Christian Science Monitor* (www.csmonitor.com). Reproduced with permission.

Heenan, David A. "An American Odyssey: The Corporate Migration to Rural America," PACNET Newsletter, Center for Strategic and International Studies, 1999.

Hoberg, Paul. E-mail interview by Chris Hansen, Champaign, IL, 2 January 2003.

Hof, Robert D. and Steve Hamm. "How E-Biz Rose, Fell and Will Rise Anew," *Business Week* (13 May 2002): 64–72.

Hueber, Betsy. Telephone interview by author, Effingham, IL, 6 January 2003.

Jackson County, IN. Survey by author, Effingham, IL, 2002.

Karlgaard, Rich. "Boonyack Comeback," *Forbes* (15 April 2002): 39. Reprinted by permission of *Forbes* Magazine, © 2002 Forbes, Inc.

Karlgaard, "Small-Jet Shocker," *Forbes* (15 September 2003): 35.

"Kmart Delisted After 84 Years on Big Board," www.foxnews.com, 19 December 2002.

Roberson, Roger. Telephone interview by author, Effingham, IL, 7 January 2003.

Ross, Marilyn and Tom. *Country Bound: Trade in Your Business Suit Blues for Blue Jean Dreams.* Buena Vista: Communication Creativity, 1997.

Schulz, John D. "Wanted: Reconfiguration," *TrafficWorld* (9 June 2003): 9.

Shedd, Randall. E-mail from Jason Wright, 17 December 2002.

Tully, Shawn. "Straighten Up and Fly Right," *Fortune* (17 February 2003): 70.

Walton, Sam and John Huey. *Sam Walton: Made in America—My Story.* New York: Doubleday, 1992.

www.bluelight.com, Kmart Corporation

www.conocophillips.com, ConocoPhillips

www.dreamtowns.com, Dreamtowns.com

www.glenwoodsprings.net, Glenwood Springs Chamber Resort Association

www.thomastonchamber.com, Thomaston-Upson Chamber of Commerce

www.uprr.com, Union Pacific Corporation

www.walmart.com, Wal-Mart Stores, Inc.

www.workfromanywhere.com, The Telework Coalition

Chapter Three

Baker, Don. Interview by author, Effingham, IL, 2002.

Bauer, Bill. Interview by author, Effingham, IL, 2002.

Bigelow, Susan. Survey by author, Effingham, IL, 2002.

Escapule, Dusty. Interview by author, Effingham, IL, 2002.

Fitzgerald, Sharon H. *Powerhouse of the West: Images of Gillette-Campbell County, WY* (2002 edition).

Howard, Bob. Interview by Lisa Huston, Effingham, IL 8 January 2003.

Koch, Barbara. Interview by Todd Thoman, Effingham IL, 2002.

Price, Ted. *Miracle Town: Creating America's Bavarian Village in Leavenworth, Washington.* Vancouver: Price & Rodgers, 1997.

Ruben, Bonnie Miller. "Quite a Ride for TREK," *Chicago Tribune* (23 January 2003), Business Section.

Thomas, Lois. *Blue Ribbon for Growth: Images of Douglas-Coffee County, GA* (2001 edition). Published by Journal Communications, Inc.

Wathen, Greg. Interview by the author, Effingham IL, 2002.

www.cityofwaverly.net, City of Waverly, OH

www.leavenworth.org, Leavenworth Chamber of Commerce

www.natat.org, National Association of Towns and Townships

www.smallcommunities.org, National Center for Small Communties

www.swidc.org, Southwest Indiana Development Council

Chapter Four

Gurwitt, Rob. "Light in Oxford: How the Vision of One Independent Bookseller Has Revitalized the Heart of Faulkner's Mississippi," *Mother Jones* (May/June 2000).

Hamilton, Scott T. Survey by author, Effingham, IL, 2002.

Johnson, Hillary. "The Economy of Modernism: How Architecture Inspires Pride and Creates Jobs in Columbus, IN," *Worth* (July/August 2000).

Nickell, Joe Ashbrook. "Mayberry DSL," *Business 2.0* (August 2002): 17–18.

Parker, Suzi. "New Economy Recasts the Rural South," *The Christian Science Monitor* (3 May 2000).

Powell, Shirley. Interview by Lisa Huston, Effingham, IL, 7 January 2003.

Rinker, Kathryn. E-mail interview by Coleen Phillips, Effingham, IL, 2 October 2002.

Stanley, Rick. E-mail interview by Lisa Huston, Effingham, IL, 19 February 2003.

Sweets, Ellen. "Oxford's Charms Survive Its Turbulent Past," *The Dallas Morning News* (17 March 2002).

www.assetpub.com, Asset International, Inc.

www.columbus.in.us, Columbus Area Visitors Center

www.co.york.me.us, York County, ME

www.cummins.com, Cummins, Inc.

www.decaturtx.org, City of Decatur, TX

www.decaturtx.com, Decatur Chamber of Commerce

www.effinghamil.org, City of Effingham, IL

www.fortpayne.com, Fort Payne Chamber of Commerce

www.mainstreet.org, National Trust for Historic Preservation's National Main Street Center

www.partners.ms/downtowners/index.htm, Picayune-Downtowners Association

www.thomasvillega.com, Thomasville-Thomas County Historic Plantations Convention and Visitors Bureau

www.wakullacounty.com, Wakulla County, FL

www.walldrug.com, Wall Drug Store

Yager, Mike. Interview by author, Effingham, IL, 2002.

Chapter Five

"A Fading State: Fare Thee Well, Iowa," *The Economist* (18 August 2001): 23–24.

Adams, Josh. "Door Wide Open," *SAIL* (March 2002): 90–91, 93–95.

Carder, Norma. Interview by Lisa Huston, Effingham, IL, 2002.

Dunn, Jr., Jerry Camarillo et al. *National Geographic Guide to Small Town Escapes*. National Geographic Society, 2002.

Fitzpatrick, Dale. Interview by author, Effingham, IL, 2002.

Fraser, Charles E. As quoted in *Southern Living*. © 2003, *Southern Living*. Reprinted with permission.

Galvez, Tara. E-mail interview by Lisa Huston, Effingham, IL, 18 December 2002.

Greider, Tarah. "CNN's Larry Smith to Serve as 2002 SOFF Special Guest," *ICTC People* (15 July 2002).

Lounsbury, Helen. "City with a Spark," *The Bay City Times*.

Martin, Douglas. "Charles E. Fraser, 73, Dies; Developer of Hilton Head," *The New York Times* (19 December 2002).

Samuel, David. Interview by author, Effingham, IL, 2002.

Schaeffer, Willy. As quoted on www.vail.snow.com. © 2003, Vail Resorts, Inc.

Sur, Larry. Interview by author, Effingham, IL, 2002.

Tamberrino, Frank. Survey by author, Effingham, IL, 2002.

Villani, John. *The 100 Best Small Art Towns in America: Discover Creative Communities, Fresh Air, and Affordable Living.* Emeryville: Avalon Travel Publishing, 1998.

www.baynavigator.com, Businesses in the Appalachicola Bay Area

www.beaufortarts.com, The Arts Council of Beaufort County

www.beauforttraveler.com, *Beaufort Traveler*

www.bgivb.com, Brunswick-Golden Isles Visitors Bureau

www.cr.nps.gov/nr/travel/amana/intro.htm, National Park Service

www.bizbuilder.org, Lincoln Trail eCommerce Enterprises, Inc.

www.cityofliberal.com, Liberal Convention and Tourism Bureau

www.cityofsandpoint.com, City of Sandpoint, ID

www.clarkstonchamber.org, Clarkston Chamber of Commerce

www.cmog.org, Corning Museum of Glass

www.corningny.com, City of Corning, NY

www.dawson.org, Dawson County Chamber of Commerce

www.discovernewporttn.com, Father & Son Marketing

www.golfcapitaltn.com, Crossville-Cumberland County Chamber of Commerce

www.grantspass.com, City of Grants Pass, OR

www.greeneville.com, Excalibur Data Solutions, Inc.

www.hanmo.com, G3 Business Innovations

www.hannibal.com, Hannibal.com

www.hhisleinfo.com, Hilton Head Island, SC Information Site

www.hillsborochamber.org, Hillsboro Area Chamber of Commerce

www.hiltonheadchamber.com, Hilton Head Island-Bluffton Chamber of Commerce

www.hindustantimes.com, Hindustan Times, Ltd.

www.kalispellchamber.com, Kalispell, MT Chamber of Commerce

www.lake-placid.ny.us, City of Lake Placid, NY

www.lakesunleader.com, *The Lake Sun Leader*, Camdenton, MO

www.parkcityinfo.com, Park City Chamber of Commerce & Visitors Bureau

www.prescott.org, Prescott, AZ Chamber of Commerce

www.rogueweb.com/gpass, Rogue Web of Southern Oregon

www.sanjuanisland.org, San Juan Island Chamber of Commerce

www.tetonwyo.org, Teton County, WY

www.und.edu/news/messages/.737.html, University of North Dakota-Grand Forks

www.usu.edu, Utah State University

www.visitamishcountry.com, Holmes County Chamber of Commerce

www.whitehouse.gov/history/presidents, U.S. Government

www2.cr.nps.gov, Heritage Preservation Services, National Park Service

Zimmerman, Fred and Dave Beal. *2002 Manufacturing Works: The Vital Link Between Production and Prosperity.* Chicago: Dearborn Trade Publishing, 2002.

Chapter Six

Buffalo County-Community Health Partners. *2002 Report to the Community.* Kearney, NE, 2002.

Buley, Bill. "Bob Potter: Mr. Jobs Plus, Retirement Doesn't Suit Salesman," *The Press* (27 January 2002).

Cayford, Tracey. E-mail interview by Coleen Phillips, Effingham, IL, 16 September 2002.

Hand in Hand: Community and Economic Development in Tupelo. The Aspen Institute, 1999.

Jackson, Phil and Hugh Delehanty. *Sacred Hoops: Spiritual Lessons of a Hardwood Warrior.* New York: Hyperion, 1995. Reprinted by permission of Hyperion.

Jaxon, Jay. As quoted on www.cnn.com, 20 October 2002.

McDonald, Tommy. Survey by author, Effingham, IL, 2002.

Rumbarger, David. Interview by author, Effingham, IL, 31 December 2002.

Senge, Peter. "Creating Quality Communities," in Kazimerez Gozdz's *Community Building, Renewing Spirit and Learning in Business.* San Francisco: New Leaders Press, 1995. Reference from Moxley, Russ S., *Leadership and Spirit.* San Francisco: Jossey-Bass Inc., 2000.

Spira, Caroline. Survey by author, Effingham, IL, 30 April 2002.

Wilgoren, Jodi. "Bond with New York is Felt in Fire-Truck-Building Town," *The New York Times* (30 November 2001).

Williams, Mark. Interview by Todd Thoman, Effingham, IL, 20 December 2002.

www.barrychamber.com/leadership.htm, The Barry County Area Chamber of Commerce

www.chiltoncountychamber.com, Chilton County Chamber of Commerce

www.colville.com/aboutcol.htm, Colville Chamber of Commerce

www.dced.utah.gov, Utah Department of Community and Economic Development

www.gctelegram.com, *The Garden City Telegram*

www.hammond.org, City of Hammond, LA

Chapter Seven

Heath, Richard. *Bittersweet: The Story of the Heath Candy Co.* West Frankfurt: New Authors Publications, Inc., 1995.

Koch, Will. Interview by Lisa Huston, Santa Claus, IN, 9 August 2002.

Lieb, Bobby. Interview by author, Effingham, IL 2002.

Woo, Vivian and Shlomo Reifman. "Private Business," *Forbes* (24 November 2003): 174–216.

www.cabelas.com, Cabela's, Inc.

www.farmlandinfo.org, American Farmland Trust

www.holidayworld.com, Holiday World and Splashin' Safari

www.wgyates.com, W.G. Yates & Sons Construction Co.

Chapter Eight

Benoit, Paul. Interview by author, Effingham, IL, 2002.

Federal Reserve Bank. *Economic Review* (Second Quarter 2003).

Forrester, Stephen. Interview by author, Effingham, IL, 2 January 2003.

Hunnicutt, Jack. Interview by author, Effingham, IL, 10 March 2003.

Jenison, Kevin. Interview by author, Effingham, IL, 31 December 2002.

Lumpkin, Richard. Interview by author, Effingham, IL, 2002.

Moore, Darrell. Interview by author, Effingham, IL, 14 February 2003.

"SIUE School of Business Announces Business of Year Awards:
    Six Family Businesses from Variety of Sectors Recognized for
    Excellence in Community Impact," *Illinois Business Report*
    (December 2002).
Sullivan, Dave. Interview by author, Effingham, IL, 31 December 2002.
Wright, Jason. Interview by Coleen Phillips, Effingham, IL, 17
    December 2002.
www.deathtax.com, *The Seattle Times*

Chapter Nine

"The breakfast of champions," Wheaties, General Mills, Inc.
Fauver, Jeff. Interview by author, Effingham, IL, 6 December 2002.
Franklin, Stephen. *Three Strikes: Labor's Heartland Losses and What They
    Mean for Working Americans.* New York: The Guilford Press, 2001.
"Good to the last drop", Maxwell House, Kraft Foods, Inc.
"It's The Real Thing," The Coca-Cola Company
"Just do it," a trademark of Nike, Inc. and its affiliates. Used by permission.
"Like a Rock," Chevrolet, General Motors Corporation
Sheckler Finch, Jackie. "Island of Yesterday," *American Profile* (11 May
    2002): 8.
www.bisbeearizona.com, Bisbee Chamber of Commerce
www.cityofwhitewater.com, Whitewater Community Development
    Authority
www.co.blaine.id.us, Blaine County, ID
www.hammond.org, City of Hammond, LA
www.hardycountywv.com, Hardy County, WV
www.mackinac.com, Mackinac.com
www.mynevadacounty.com, County of Nevada, CA
www.ok-corral.com, OK Corral
www.prescott.org, Prescott, AZ Chamber of Commerce
www.sgcity.org, City of St. George, UT
www.smallcommunities.org, National Center for Small Communities
www.smallcommunities.org/ncsc/THN.htm, National Center for
    Small Communities

Chapter Ten

Associated Press. "Adelphia to move corporate headquarters to
  Denver," *The New York Times* (29 January 2003): C6.
Barrett, John. As quoted on www.cnn.com, 22 September 2000.
Hanna, Karna. Interview by Lisa Huston, Effingham, IL, 28 February
  2003.
Jonsson, Patrik. "A Textile Town Reinvents Itself as NASCAR's Mecca,"
  The Christian Science Monitor (15 April 2002).
Kramer, Tommy. Interview by Todd Thoman, Chicago, IL, 2002.
Leonard, Devin. "The Adelphia Story," *Fortune* (12 August 2002).
McBride, Jennifer. "Badger history revisited," *Baraboo News Gazette*
  (18 March 2002).
Sharnberg, Kirsten. "Empty Plant, Empty Pockets," *Chicago Tribune* (9
  July 2002).
www.comsprague.com, Commonwealth Sprague
www.guymoncofc.com/rodeofacts.htm, Guymon, OK Chamber of
  Commerce
www.northcarolinaspeedway.com, North Carolina Motor Speedway
www.ptc.com, PTC Solutions
www.scdc.com, Sauk County Development Corporation
www.villageprofile.com/iowa/charlescity/02his/topic.html,
  Community Profile Network, Inc.

Chapter Eleven

Blattner, Tim. Interview by author, Effingham, IL, 12 February 2003.
Cairo Public Library, Cairo, IL
Cape Girardeau Chamber of Commerce 1997 Membership Directory. Cape
  Girardeau: Cape Girardeau Chamber of Commerce, 1996.
Knudtson, Jay. Interview by author, Cape Girardeau, MO, 17
  December 2002.
Miller, Mike. Interview by author, Cape Girardeau, MO, 17 December
  2002.
Ross, David. Interview by author, Cape Girardeau, MO, 17 December
  2002.

Rust, Gary. Interview by author, Cape Girardeau, MO, 17 December 2002.

www.capechamber.com, Cape Girardeau Chamber of Commerce

www.capegirardeaucvb.org, Cape Girardeau Convention and Visitors Bureau

www.cityofcapegirardeau.org, City of Cape Girardeau, MO

www.cityofcapegirardeau.org/condev/vision2020/survey.htm, City of Cape Girardeau, MO

www.semoport.com, Southeast Missouri Regional Port Authority

Wyman, John and Jerri Wyman. Interview by author, Cape Girardeau, MO, 17 December 2002.

Chapter Twelve

www.bransonchamber.com, Branson/Lakes Area Chamber of Commerce and Convention & Visitors Bureau

www.homefair.com, National Association of Realtors

www.milkeninstitute.com, Milken Institute

Appendices

"A Portrait of Carson City, Douglas and Storey Counties," Reno: Sierra Pacifica Economic Development Department, 1999.

Bylinsky, Gene. "Closing in on Perfection," *Fortune* (23 June 2003).

Community Profile, Traverse City Area Chamber of Commerce, Traverse City, MO, 2002.

Everett, Karen. Survey by author, Effingham, IL, 2002.

Fox, Richard L., ed. *America's Best Places to Retire.* Houston: Vacation Publications, Inc., 2002.

Kraft, Ron. Survey by author, Effingham, IL, 19 April 2002.

Petersen, John. Interview by author, Effingham, IL, 15 August 2002.

"Yours to Enjoy," Snow Hill: Worcester County Tourism Office (September 2000).

www.alicepeckday.org, Alice Peck Day Memorial Hospital

www.berkeleysprings.com, Travel Berkeley Springs, Inc.

www.bev.net, The Blacksburg Electronic Village

www.bozemancvb.visitmt.com, Bozeman Convention and Visitors'
   Bureau
www.ci.bend.or.us, City of Bend, OR
www.cooperstownchamber.org, Cooperstown Chamber of Commerce
www.corvettemuseum.com, National Corvette Museum
www.dallasfed.org/research/busfront/bus0202.html, Federal Reserve
   Bank of Dallas
www.dhmc.org, Dartmouth-Hitchcock Medical Center
www.gostowe.com, Stowe Area Association
www.greencastle.com, Greencastle, IN
www.hollisterrealty.com, Vedana Freitas, RE/MAX PLATINUM
   PROPERTIES
www.hotmusic.org/abouthsmf.htm, Hot Springs Music Festival
www.indianriverchamber.com, Indian River County Chamber of
   Commerce
www.isupark.org, Iowa State University Research Park Corporation
www.kitty-hawk.com, Kitty Hawk, NC
www.mauryregional.com, Maury Regional Healthcare System
www.mtnhome.net, Mountain Home, AR
www.nces.ed.gov, National Center for Education Statistics
www.nhis.com, New Hampshire International Speedway
www.northga.net/whitfield/outlet.html, North Georgia, USA
www.ococean.com, Department of Tourism, Ocean City, MD
www.poconoraceway.com, Pocono International Raceway
www.rochestermn.com, Rochester, MN
www.saintcroixriver.com, St. Croix Riverway
www.seaportgeorgetown.com, Historic Seaport Georgetown, SC
www.smuckers.com, The J.M. Smucker Co.
www.spacityblues.com, Spa City Blues Society
www.saturn.com, Saturn Corporation
www.sundance.org, Sundance Film Festival
www.talladegasuperspeedway.com, Talladega Superspeedway
www.taoschamber.org, Taos County Chamber of Commerce
www.txcoastalbend.org, Texas Coastal Bend Regional Tourism Council
www.utahreach.usu.edu/sanpete/visitor/index.htm, UtahReach
www.villageprofile.com/illinois/mattoon/matoon2.html, Community
   Profile Network

Contact Information for Jack Schultz

For updates on Boomtown USA's agurbs and to sign up for a free
e-newsletter, please visit www.boomtownusa.net or www.agurbs.com.

For information on booking Mr. Schultz as a speaker, e-mail
speak@boomtownusa.net or speak@agurbs.com.